# The Winning Golf Swing: Simple Technical Solutions for Lower Scores

## Kristian Baker

BENNION
KEARNY

Published in 2017 by Bennion Kearny Limited.

Copyright © Bennion Kearny Ltd 2017

ISBN: 978-1-910515-11-2

Published by Bennion Kearny Limited
6 Woodside
Churnet View Road
Oakamoor
ST10 3AE

www.BennionKearny.com


Photos: Bob Atkins | Golfer: David Griffiths

# About the Author

Kristian Baker is the Head of Instruction at The Wentworth Club in Surrey where he has worked for over 20 years.

Kristian has compiled an impressive CV of coaching results and has worked with club members, leading amateurs, and some of the best professionals in the world. The professionals have competed on the US and European Tour, winning numerous European Tour events including the European Open, Dutch Open and the St Omer Open. Kristian's most notable professional results, to date, came during his years coaching Ross Fisher. He began coaching Ross whilst he was still an amateur at Wentworth before establishing himself as one of the world's best professional players.

Kristian has taught several other European Tour players who have also won on the European Tour. Amateurs he has coached have won many of the top events including the English Amateur, Faldo World Series and Finnish Amateur, amongst others.

kristianbaker.com | @kgbgolf

# Acknowledgements

This book is a thank you to all of the golfers who I've been fortunate enough to teach for the past 20 years at The Wentworth Club. Without allowing me to help you with your golf, I would never have had so much enjoyment from the game and learnt so much about coaching.

To all of the hugely talented professionals with whom I've been so fortunate to meet and learn so much from – your generosity (not just with your time but also the sharing of your knowledge) will be forever appreciated.

A special thank you must go to the people who have helped make this book possible: Chris Sells – StrokeAverage.com, Karl Morris – The Mind Factor, Mark Bull – Bull3D, Emanuel Frauenlob – TrackMan Golf, Bertie Cordle – DST Golf, and my publisher James Lumsden-Cook – Bennion Kearny. Your time, patience, and willingness to answer my constant questions, at all hours of the day and night for the past two years, is truly appreciated. In turn, I would like to express my gratitude to David Griffiths for his excellent and patient(!) work as the golfer who you see photographed across this book.

Finally, to all of my friends and family, especially my wife Rebecca, son Alex, and parents Bob and Barbara; without your love and support, I wouldn't have been able to undertake the many things that I have been fortunate enough to achieve.

# About the Contributors

**Chris Sells** started working as the official golf analyst for the English Golf Union in 2001. Sixteen years ago, he conceived the StrokeAverage.com approach to game improvement, and over time his reputation has grown to the point where he is now regarded by peers as a leading contributor to the game of golf, with a full understanding of how to support players in becoming winners.

He was a key part of Paul McGinley's winning 2014 Ryder Cup team providing Paul with data analysis before and during the tournament. He works with, and has worked with, players at the top of their game on the European Tour, PGA Tour, LET and LPGA. The StrokeAverage.com client list speaks for itself. To find out more about Chris and StrokeAverage.com go to *www.chrissellsgolf.com* or *www.strokeaverage.com*

*

**Karl Morris** is one of Europe's leading Performance Coaches who has worked with, and achieved success with, six Major winners and over 100 PGA Tour, European Tour, LPGA and Ladies European Tour golfers.

He has built an enviable reputation as someone who helps players to get the best out of their abilities, no matter what the level. He has consistently produced outstanding results for clients at all levels of sport (and business) with a practical and applicable approach, based on real world experience as opposed to classroom theory.

Karl has also provided consultancy to the PGA of Great Britain and Europe and he has presented seminars to the Australian PGA, South African PGA, German PGA, Swedish PGA, Dutch PGA, Belgian PGA, GUI and the Hong Kong Golf Association, to name but a few.

*

**TrackMan** is a fully wireless, easy to use, indoor/outdoor, radar-based solution for analysing impact conditions and resulting ball flight in golf. Their technologies are trusted by all the major stakeholders in the game with more than 700 tour professionals, thousands of coaches, fitters, and amateurs, as well as all major equipment manufacturers, and broadcasters relying on TrackMan's accurate data to analyse performance and talent. Founded in 2003 and headquartered in Vedbæk, Denmark, the company holds a comprehensive patent portfolio of granted patents and pending patents applications.

*

**Bertie Cordle** is the founder and CEO of DST Golf. He has invented ground-breaking technology which enables a golfer to Locate, Train and Perfect the Optimal Impact Position, the position in which the club shaft is under tension and the club head under control at impact. This technology is used in DST's training clubs, the DST Compressor and the CR-10. Bertie was formerly a tour professional and has since worked alongside more than 300 PGA & European Tour players, assisting them and their swing coaches.

# Foreword

I am delighted Kristian Baker has decided to write this book on the golf swing. Also, I am honoured to be asked to write the foreword.

Kristian is a PGA professional, based at Wentworth Club for the past 20 years. He is passionate about teaching and helping players of all standards to achieve their full potential, including my son Jamie!

The teaching methods as explained in the book are uncomplicated, easy-to-understand and are based on time-proven fundamentals whilst also incorporating modern science and technology. I believe Kristian's book offers much more than many modern day golf books because of its broader content.

Kristian is a highly regarded member of the Wentworth golf staff and has played a major role in the successful Golf Scholarship Scheme at the Club. Ryder Cup Player Ross Fisher and others have achieved national and international success through this renowned initiative.

Reading the book will not necessarily guarantee Ryder Cup status to all, however by applying Kristian's methods and ideas I am confident the reader will become a better player.

**Bernard Gallacher, O.B.E.**

# Table of Contents

# Introduction

What do you have in common with Rory McIlroy, Justin Rose, Jordan Spieth, Lydia Ko, and Jason Day? You are all looking for that 'something' which makes you the best you can be, and which gives you the greatest opportunity for success.

Every golfer, at every level, seeks knowledge on how to improve – and this book will help you do that. This book draws upon both my experiences, and those of established golf professionals and experts I have worked with, and summarises our knowledge in a format to help you improve.

If you are a tour player wanting to move into the top 50, a professional wanting to secure a tour card, or an amateur wanting to compete better in club competitions – this is the book for you.

## Coaching winning

So, how do you get better at golf?

Now, that's a very interesting question and one that many golfers ask themselves on a weekly basis. In turn, if there were a simple answer, we would all be competing for that top spot!

To start with, I'm going to make one very big assumption, namely that becoming a better golfer means you want to score lower. This will seem like a very obvious statement to many but, for a few, getting better might just be hitting it straighter, longer, or just 'liking' the look of their golf swing.

Essentially, as a coach, I want to help a student achieve all of these things. For me, though, the biggest measure of success (and by far the most important and enjoyable part) is seeing players score lower. We may often play for the pure pleasure of the game but, even under these circumstances, most players are looking to go around the course in as few shots as possible. Competitive or not, does anyone really enjoy playing a poor round of golf? That is the challenge of the game – to always be better than before. In order to coach a player to achieve this, there needs to be a system. We will come to this system, in detail, shortly.

In order to reinforce my teaching, and cement understanding, I aim to offer as much scientific, factual evidence as possible. Evidence-based coaching is, in my view, the most effective way to coach.

"If you can't measure it, you can't coach it." Sir Clive Woodward, England Rugby's World Cup Winning Coach.

This is a great phrase and resonates strongly with my view and experience of coaching over the last 20 years. If we don't accurately know and understand what has actually happened… it's impossible to apply the correct fix.

We can only guess. And why guess, when you can measure? Know yourself, know your game, and know your strategy for improving.

For many years, I have successfully used three key resources to secure game improvement.

1. Statistics.
2. Complete ball flight and club tracking through impact.
3. Biomechanics.

Over the course of this book, I will introduce you to each area in turn.

## This book

This book is designed to help in two key situations. Firstly, when you are alone, either playing on the course or on the practice ground. Secondly, when you are taking a lesson.

The definition of insanity is "doing the same thing over and over and expecting different results," said Albert Einstein. Unfortunately, many golfers play or practice golf the same way, time after time. They keep making the same mistakes, hoping a consistent, better result will happen magically. Crazy!

There is no doubt that the best way to improve is to get a lesson off a reputable coach; their experience allows them to assess your game and offer practical ways to improve. However, the more understanding and knowledge a golfer has about his or her technique, strengths, and weaknesses, the more able the golfer is to help themselves.

So, this book is designed to help you acquire knowledge about the correct golf swing and impact laws. Essentially, it is about you taking ownership (through knowledge) of your game. Firstly, it means you can correct your wayward shots when on the course or practice tee alone (no coach or radar).

Secondly, when you do have a lesson, you will be far better equipped to understand and internalise information, leading to the quickest possible improvement.

Imagine, if you have hit a bad shot off the first tee, having the knowledge to evaluate the ball flight, know what happened at impact, what was likely to be the primary swing fault that caused it, and how to fix it!

I'm confident that with knowledge and understanding, you will be able to understand your poor shots and fix your swing in a far shorter time than from hitting hundreds of balls, guessing what the problem is, and hoping to stumble upon the right solution.

## The system

My system for fixing golf shots starts before I see a shot hit. The first part is the player's game make-up, by which I mean 'how' they are constructing their scores. Ideally, this will be based on numbers and taken from a stats report. I'll explain this in more detail later in the book.

A score is created from a number of elements which are derived from one another. The top line element is the shot (that's what ultimately creates our score), but it is a result of primary factors (what happens at impact between the club head and ball), which is a result of references (preferred swing technique).

So, our system looks like this:

**Score / Statistics**
Factual evidence of the golfer's game

*[derived from]*

**Shot**
The flight of a ball

↓

**Primary factor**
What happened at impact between
the club and the ball

↓

**References**
Preferred swing technique

By using the system in this order, it should be simple to diagnose a fault and be precise in applying the correct fix.

Let's get started!

# Chapter 1
# Stats – What YOU need to know

## Stats hold your scoring secrets

'Stats' is a term that we hear more and more often in golf; especially when we watch golf on TV or look at tour websites. But why are so many of the world's best players recording and analysing their stats? And, perhaps more importantly, why should you bother? Can it actually make a difference to your game?

For the past 15 years, I've been fascinated by golf stats and what they can offer. In turn, I have been fortunate enough to work alongside the best in the world at interpreting them.

There are some people in life who are 'moved' by statistics, Chris Sells of *StrokeAverage.com* is one of these people. Being in the golf stats business since 2001, I'd like to introduce you to Chris as he has conceived a unique formula that allows 'the numbers' of golf to be translated into a truly effective game improvement tool. Indeed, it is a tool that is highly regarded by elite players across the world including Rory McIlroy, Graeme McDowell, Chris Wood, Rafa Cabrera Bello, Brooks Koepka, Lydia Ko, and Stacy Lewis to name but a few. Chris uses this tool to support players with strategies for game improvement, and *his success* is borne out by the achievements of his clients.

At first glance, stats can appear to be a collection of numbers or data. They are, however, the very DNA of a golfer's game; the first reference point we should look at when trying to improve our scores. This is why stats are front and centre (and the first chapter) in this book.

Stats are crucial in helping a golfer:

1. Understand their game
2. Determine a plan to maximize their ability; getting better by building their game around their strengths and weaknesses

Effectively, what you are doing is keeping an accurate record of what you *intended* to do with a shot and what the *end result* was. Do this for all your shots during a round and a pattern will emerge. Once the data has been correctly analysed, a plan can be put into place for improving your scores.

The main issue a golfer has when trying to understand their game – *if they do not keep stats* – is that everything boils down to perception and opinion. And when it does, because our thinking is fallible, we get things wrong and often come to poor conclusions. This is because emotion plays a large part in shaping our perceptions (especially with regard to a player's most recent round). It is often human nature, for example, to focus on what we 'see' as negative elements to our game even though they might not be. We then waste our time on improving these elements when we should be focusing on other things.

Without objective analysis, a player can be way off the mark when identifying actual strengths and weaknesses. They can go in completely the wrong direction when trying to improve!

## Avoid the trap, too many golfers get it wrong

A player is convinced that he tends to drive to the left and as a result spends many hours practicing to rectify this issue through a swing change. Importantly, his conviction becomes reinforced by his apparent lack of success in rectifying the issue. But it turns out that drives to the left are caused by a club defect. Whilst practice might have developed skills to reduce this, all the practicing in the world is unlikely to resolve it properly. Often, an 'emotional conclusion' regarding drives to the left might convince a player that this problem occurs with more than just the one club. The stats would show that it is just **one** particular club where the problem arises, and therefore the club is the issue... not technique.

It is well documented that at the end of 2012, the then World No. 1, Rory McIlroy, switched equipment from Titleist to Nike. Many people (including Nick Faldo) speculated that it could be a dangerous move and it is fair to say he had a fairly mixed or slow start to the year. Chris Sells was analysing the stats on Rory and contrary to public opinion, his mid-season report for Rory and his support team highlighted that a number of his clubs were actually better than for the previous year. However, the report also highlighted/confirmed that there were just a few more errant tee shots happening with his Driver (e.g. they were going into fairway bunkers, bushes, or resulting in penalties; plus there was a tendency to drive to the right more than normal). Based on this analysis, Chris highlighted a potential issue with the driver. Following further equipment testing with Nike and prior to the British Open, Rory switched to a new prototype Driver and over the subsequent months his driving improved. This had the desired knock-on effect to his scoring in 2014, and he climbed back to World No. 1.

Another example (illustrating how emotional responses can impact thinking) might be that a player sees the need to improve their bunker shots as key to their game. This is because they rarely recall hitting bunker shots close to the hole. Actually, their bunker play is okay (as the stats would show) and they are simply hitting too many shots into bunkers! Therefore, the player thinks they need to improve this area whereas, in reality, they first need to understand and correct why they are causing so many bunker shots. This can be due to course management mistakes, mental errors, or technical swing issues. Accepting what the stats are telling you can sometimes be a challenge if you have another view in mind.

As a side note, it is important to recognise that huge confidence can come from knowing your strengths. These can sometimes contradict perceptions. It's wrong to think of stats as only focusing on the negatives; we must recognize the positive information they can offer. That way, we build the complete picture of our game.

I hope, from the above, that you can see why it's essential to keep data on every shot you hit. From the data and subsequent analysis, specific areas can be highlighted and will impact other areas. Combine all of this together, and that's how you can quickly look to reduce your scores.

The process of improvement is continuous as you can see from the illustration below:

# How to collect statistics in golf

Collecting the correct data, and ensuring it is accurate, is crucial to game improvement. If the data we collect is inaccurate then it can be highly destructive; we need it to be an exact reflection of the rounds that we have played. There are various ways you can collect your stats:

- Writing them down manually

- Entering them into computer software

- Using technology attached to your clubs that recognizes when and where you hit shots from (this technology will upload data to mobile devices over the course of a round)

# What you need to know

This first information we need is what equipment was used: woods, irons, wedges, putter, and ball. Should any of it change at any point, it should be noted. That includes a completely new club you've added or just a new grip. An ongoing record of your equipment is crucial.

The club that you use for each shot needs to be seen as an individual. You may have matching woods or irons, but a minor defect in any one of them can cause an issue. Alongside this, it's always useful to note if anything else that could be seen as equipment has been added or dropped. This could be range finders, green reading charts, an electric trolley versus carrying your bag, etc. Additionally, it's important to note who is in the team of the player and if this changes. This would include a swing coach, biomechanist, short game coach, putting coach, performance coach, fitness coach, physio, etc.

Next, you need to collect data from the course. Other than the hole number, length of the hole, and its par, I would suggest you also record:

- What club you hit

- Your intention behind the tee shot (i.e. attempting to hit the green or not)

- Was your shot an advancing shot (i.e. a chip out of the trees back onto the fairway)

- What type of shot were you playing (normal/chip/pitch/lob)

- Where (direction-wise) did the ball finish relevant to where you intended

- What was the finishing lie of the ball (fairway/bunker/semi-rough/rough/bushes-trees/water hazard/out of bounds/greenside bunker/fringe/green)

- Were any penalty shots taken

- Shot lengths or putt lengths

As previously mentioned, the accuracy of this data is crucial. To ensure accuracy is maintained I would always recommend recording your data the same day, ideally during (or straight after) the round. The easiest way I have found to keep this information during the round (when not using a digital device) is to record the clubs you hit and the distances hit in your yardage book. Then, at the end of the day, you can easily transfer the information into a master paper record or upload this information into relevant software or a website such as StrokeAverage.com.

Recording an accurate estimate of your putt length distances is *absolutely vital*. To help ensure you record the correct lengths of putts, spend a little time with a long tape measure on the practice putting green. Guess some random lengths of putts then measure them to improve your recordings on the course. You'll be amazed at how accurate you can become at estimating distances with very little practice.

Chris Sells always makes clear to clients that recording stats shouldn't be a distraction in any way when playing. You're simply, after your round or shot, accurately recalling how you played and putting the facts into a system that can then be analysed. Typically, you would need a minimum of 15 rounds of golf before you begin to analyse any data properly. This way, you can see the patterns that have developed and any one-off outliers won't skew the information.

The correct recording and analysis of your statistics will eliminate any misconceptions or inconsistencies.

# Why you're not average

It's important to remember that everybody is unique and their games will reflect their individual elements. Therefore any assessment needs to take into account the *individual* player's strengths and also their limitations.

There's no one way to play golf, and there are multiple ways to accommodate the unique approach everybody brings to it.

One example of this is how your physique will contribute to how you play. Someone built like Rory McIlroy or Dustin Johnson has a completely different approach to that of someone who is, say, built like Justin Leonard or Luke Donald.

Shorter, accurate players are likely to have a completely different approach to others who play a power game.

Over the years, Chris has had a number of players go to him saying that the only way that they can compete on Tour is by getting longer. Typically, amateurs see this as essential to becoming a low handicapper. However, far too many good golfers have fallen foul of this misconception over the years. Understanding your game's strengths and weakness and learning to manage them to give you the best possible scores is what you should be focusing on. The table below seems to indicate that the shorter hitters seem to do okay and Jim Furyk is still 4th on the PGA Tour's Career Earnings List.

## PGA Tour Rounds below 60 compared with Driving Distance Rank

| Score | Score to Par | Player | Year | Event | Tour | Driving Distance Rank that Year |
|-------|-------------|--------|------|-------|------|-------------------------------|
| 58 | -12 | Jim Furyk | 2016 | Travelers Championship | PGA | 182 |
| 59 | -13 | Adam Hadwin | 2017 | Career Builder Open | PGA | 105 |
| 59 | -11 | Justin Thomas | 2017 | Sony Open Hawaii | PGA | 12 |
| 59 | -12 | Jim Furyk | 2013 | BMW Championship | PGA | 169 |
| 59 | -11 | Stuart Appleby | 2010 | Greenbrier Classic | PGA | 84 |
| 59 | -12 | Paul Goydos | 2010 | John Deere Classic | PGA | 185 |
| 59 | -13 | David Duval | 1999 | Bob Hope Classic | PGA | 9 |
| 59 | -13 | Chip Beck | 1991 | Las Vegas Invitational | PGA | 106 |
| 59 | -13 | Al Geiberger | 1977 | Memphis Classic | PGA | Rank Not available |
| | | | | | Average DD Rank | 106.5 |

A tournament and game preparation plan should mainly be built around an individual player's strengths not really around the strengths of his rivals – an awareness of what rivals are doing can be helpful but all too often leads to some poor decision making. This could be why many elite golfers decide not to look too closely at the leaderboard whilst competing; they focus on their own game, not someone else's.

The trend with analysis is to compare your game to the averages of other golfers. But how does this contribute to your game? We have already discussed how each person is unique and there is nobody else quite like you in the world. There might be someone with similar characteristics – height, weight, personality, etc. – but nobody exactly like you. So why assume that comparing yourself to an average will improve your game?

Another common mistake is for amateurs to compare their games and stats to that of Tour pros. Often people will look at them as a benchmark to aspire to, or work back from. This can be a mistake; most of the time the best comparison is yourself. There are many different things to consider when comparing Tour stats with amateur club stats; professional players exist in a hugely different world where the challenges are geared to *their* standard of play. A hole that is set up for professional tournament play should not be compared to a regular hole at your local course. There are many possible differences.

- Length and par of course
- Length and par of each hole
- Width of fairways
- Length/thickness of rough
- Designed or amended for modern equipment
- Number and type of hazards
- Speed and quality of greens
- Green undulation
- Flag locations
- Ball spotters and crowds to help locate balls and also tread down rough
- Bleachers and drop zones
- Internal OOB are generally very rare on tour; they are to protect club golfers
- Knowing and correctly interpreting the rules

It is possible that by comparing yourself to any number of 'averages', you can get demoralised. A coach for a very successful PGA Tour player (who is a client of Chris Sells) looked at the 'strokes gained' data, provided by the PGA Tour. The PGA statistics indicated that his tour player was significantly below the average yet, in reality, he was performing extremely successfully when taking all his game dynamics into account. Subsequently, more thorough and detailed analysis by Chris contradicted the simple comparison of averages and showed where and why he was having success.

Field averages have their place as good indicators of a particular skill, but they are not the key to delivering golfing success. You must understand your complete game and plan accordingly. It is not always about looking at the data to find out how to strengthen your weaknesses but understanding whether something needs to be strengthened at all. In turn, can other elements be improved to help reduce that particular weakness?

Consider the type of golfer you are and build your plan for improvement around that.

- *It is not solely a capacity to make great shots that makes champions, but the essential quality of making very few bad shots* – Tommy Armour
- Build your game around your strengths
- If it's not broken, don't fix it
- Successful golf is about a player's ability to execute the shot they are intending to hit

Recording the essential data and then conducting proper analysis will help to show the following, over a period of time:

**Equipment**

- Is your equipment suited to you and your game?
- Do you have any club defects?

**Mental**

- Do you play too aggressively or conservatively? I.e. are you picking the right shot/target to play?
- Do you try too hard or do you get easily distracted?
- Do you lose shots by varying your pre-shot routines?

**Fitness**

- Are you fit enough to maintain focus for 18 / 36 / 72 holes?
- Are you strong enough to play the required shots?
- Do you eat and drink properly?

**Technique**

- Are you currently making swing changes?
- Have you neglected to practice any areas of your game?
- What is your normal shot shape?
- Do you have a preferred directional miss?

**Lifestyle**

- Are you able to spend enough time practising, alongside your other responsibilities?
- Do you have any off-course issues that affect how you are performing on the course?

Sometimes the basic statistics do not reflect the adjustments required. This is where a skilled golf analyst is able to interpret the data and look for ways to develop a player's game further. Just recording your statistics is not enough, you must be able to interpret and use that information to improve your game. Once you have the correct interpretation of your stats you can begin to formulate a plan.

Below is a basic suggestion of how to allocate your practice time, but bear in mind that this is a typical suggestion and at times it will need to be tweaked to reflect recent trends in your game. Breaking your time into six sections like this ensures that all areas of the game are practised and not neglected.

## Basic Example Practice Time Allocation
## (55% Full Swing/Long Game, and 45% Short Game and Putting)

| 18% Driving | 20% Mid and Long Range Fairway & Recovery Shots | 17% Pitches & Short Irons | 5% Bunkers | 15% Greenside Chipping | 25% Putting |
|---|---|---|---|---|---|

It is also important to remember the contribution that each element makes to your game.

- It is not just about how good each individual stat is... it is about how often that stat impacts your score
- Not all statistics have the same importance (e.g. a bad putt from two feet that misses the hole isn't as destructive as a slice off the tee that goes out of bounds)
- Potential risk/rewards/pressures in golf often change as you advance down the hole
- There will always be exceptions to the rules

Data can be used to prove, or in some cases disprove, a player's emotional response to their game. Most golfers regularly regale 'highlights and lowlights' in their clubhouses around the world but how accurate are these stories and are they really that helpful?

For example, if you think you have hit an approach from say 150 yards to 10ft then miss the putt (but in reality it went to 15ft from the hole):

1. You are convincing yourself and others that you have hit a better approach than you really did [which might boost your confidence]

2. This is then offset by saying that you missed a shorter putt than you really stood over [which might knock your confidence]

3. If you get proper coaching and you tell your coach these pieces of information it is likely to impact upon their ability to give you the right advice/assistance to help improve your game in the correct area

4. Using stats with your coach enables them to work with you more efficiently and will be more likely to save you shots, time, and money

# Transforming your game

For higher handicap club golfers, it is perhaps a little easier to spot areas for improvement as there are fewer factors to consider and the potential to save shots is perhaps more significant (i.e. it is certainly easier to show a club golfer how to reduce their average scores from 90 to 85 than it is to help an elite golfer reduce their score on tour from 72 to 70).

By this we mean that:

Typically, golfers who can't break 90 will most likely need to improve significantly in all areas of their game, whereas the golfer who shoots closer to 72 will most likely have stronger aspects to their game alongside weaker facets; improvements will tend to come from improving specific areas whilst maintaining or slightly refining existing strengths. The recording of your data is the only accurate way to see and monitor this information.

To illustrate this point we can use information gathered by Dr L J Riccio, which provides useful guidelines for mid- and higher-handicapped club golfers. The data shows what the average golfer achieves:

**Score 91**

- 31% of Fairways
- 2 Greens in Regulation
- 35.7 Putts Per Round

**Score 85**

- 46% of Fairways
- 5 Greens in Regulation
- 33.7 Putts Per Round

**Score 79**

- 61% of Fairways
- 8 Greens in Regulation
- 31.7 Putts Per Round

**Score 75**

- 71% of Fairways
- 10 Greens in Regulation
- 30.3 Putts Per Round

**Score 71**

- 81% of Fairways
- 12 Greens in Regulation
- 29.0 Putts Per Round

Riccio's work indicates that if you want to reduce your average score by 2 shots then the main thing you need to plan for is hitting an extra green in regulation. His summary:

*3 greens breaks 90, 8 greens breaks 80, and 13 greens breaks 70.*

Riccio has concluded that tee to green accuracy is the key for all golfers. But this does not mean we ignore the short game and putting (they are still factors although less influential). As discussed above, the critical point is how important tee to green accuracy is for you, your individual capabilities, your style of play, and the courses you play.

Importantly, Riccio's data pattern does not apply so well to elite tour professional players:

"Although the average Tour Pro might average 71 in a season, there are not many who hit as many as 81% of fairways on a typical Tour Course, as their courses are usually tighter and longer, so their average on Tour would be nearer to 60% driving accuracy. It is important to understand here that although the Tour Pro may only hit around 60% of fairways, generally speaking, their 'miss' is much less destructive compared with club golfers and they have greater skills in terms of their recovery shots. By keeping your stats in the way described we can not only see the directional miss of your shots but also the severity of these shots."

It is, therefore, important that you understand what it is that YOU need to do to improve and where your game currently lies. It's good to be aware of average performances, but this must be done constructively rather than destructively.

Once a golfer is capable of regularly breaking 80, Chris Sells believes they should start to consider the *Effective Greens in Regulation* statistic which (alongside other helpful stats) indicates the following:

1. Overall swing efficiency and ball striking – in terms of both power and accuracy
2. Course management – shot selection
3. Short game efficiency

Chris conceived the Effective Greens in Regulation statistic in 2000, and it is far more accurate than the regular Greens in Regulation statistic. This is because it takes into account every shot played from the tee to the green. Alongside other stats, this is an extremely powerful measure of your game.

# The measures

## *Effective Greens in Regulation*

The table below shows how the Effective Greens in Regulation is calculated, the key issue being what shot was the *first* putting opportunity on each hole played, following the first successful approach or short game shot:

| First Potential Putting Opportunity | Effective GIR Points |
|---|---|
| For Albatross | 3 |
| For Eagle | 2 |
| For Birdie | 1 |
| For Par | 0 |
| For Bogey | -1 |
| For Double Bogey | -2 |
| For Triple Bogey | -3 |
| For Quadruple Bogey | -4 |
| Etc. | Etc. |

The table below is another way of looking at the scoring method above, based on the par of the hole.

| Golf Hole \| Par | 1st shot lands on Green | 2nd Shot lands on Green | 3rd shot lands on Green | 4th shot lands on Green | 5th shot lands on Green |
|---|---|---|---|---|---|
| 3 | +1 point | 0 point | -1 point | -2 points | -3 points |
| 4 | +2 points | +1 point | 0 point | -1 point | -2 point |
| 5 | +3 points | +2 points | +1 point | 0 point | -1 point |

The points for each hole are totalled at the end of the round to give an overall figure. It is possible for a player to have a higher Effective GIR than 18 (although it is quite rare) but higher handicap players might have a negative figure, and over time those golfers should be striving to improve that particular stat.

Please note: For shots that are holed from off the green, the key point remains what score would the subsequent chance have been had that shot not been holed; i.e. if a player holes his second shot on a Par 4 it still only counts as +1 Effective GIR point.

### What you can extract from this stat

Effective Greens in Regulation is a better indication of overall tee to green efficiency for the 18 holes and not just a measure of the holes that were played well. It helps to indicate whether the golfer is putting under pressure in order to score well, and further information is revealed when it is used in conjunction with the relevant putt length stats. The aim for most golfers is to increase their Effective Greens in Regulation whilst reducing their first putt lengths.

## *Scrambling*

The percentage of times the green is missed in regulation, but a par or birdie is still scored.

As an example, you play four holes of golf. On the first and second hole, you do not hit the green in regulation but still manage to score a par on each hole. On the third and fourth holes, again you do not hit the green in regulation but this time you go on to make a bogey on each hole. Your Scrambling for the four holes is 50.0%.

### What does the scrambling stat tell us

This stat essentially shows how effectively a golfer is able to recover from missing the green in regulation. It's fair to say that if you are regularly having to 'scramble' then you'll be placing huge pressure on this area of your game and it is likely to fail at some point. You are almost certain to face some scrambling situations – the best golfers in the world typically have between 4 and 6 scramble attempts per round – but we need to understand how often it's occurring. If it is too often, then we can look back and examine why greens are being missed and take actions to reduce this.

### What you can extract (or learn) from this stat

- What your course management is like (i.e. you can see if you're being too aggressive/defensive with your approach play)
- If your tee shots are making it difficult for you to scramble as you have too many penalty shots or chip outs meaning that it is more difficult to scramble
- Which types of shot around the green are more successful
- Understanding whether it is your greenside short game shots or putting that needs to improve

## Sub-Regulation Attempts per Round

The average number of times per round (also displayed as a percentage) when an attempt is made to hit the green (of the golf hole being played) in three or more shots lower than the par of the hole. So, if you attempt to hit the green in one shot on a Par 4 hole, two or fewer shots on a Par 5 hole or, three or fewer shots on a Par 6 hole, you are attempting to hit the green in sub-regulation. As an example, you play two rounds of golf; on the first round, you attempt to hit the green in sub-regulation three times and, on the second round, you attempt to hit the green in sub-regulation four times. Your Sub-Regulation Attempts *per Round* for the two rounds is 3.50.

### What does the Sub-Regulation Attempts per Round stat tell us

The main insights from sub-regulation attempts concern a player's course management. Are you playing to hit the green in sub-regulation too often and therefore having too aggressive a course management plan? Or are you not attempting to hit a green in sub-regulation when your game is good enough (and you should, therefore, be taking more attempts)?

If you are making too many inappropriate attempts, you are putting pressure on yourself. This will likely lead to failures which will cause disappointment and frustration. This may have a knock-on effect on your next shot choice. Misses from these longer clubs could ultimately turn out to be more destructive than if you had laid up with your second shot.

Alternatively, if you are in a position to reach the green off the tee, but choose not to, then you are giving away a great opportunity. With stats data, you will have the evidence to show (and therefore know) that you have the ability to hit accurate long clubs and derive confidence to play green-bound shots.

## Sub-Regulation Accuracy per Round

The average number of times per round that the golf ball finishes either in the hole or on the green (of the hole being played) in three or more shots lower than the par of the hole (also displayed as a percentage).

So, if your ball finishes on the green in one shot on a Par 4 hole, two or fewer shots on a Par 5 hole, or three or fewer shots on a Par 6 hole, you are deemed to have hit the green in sub-regulation. As an example, you play two rounds of golf; on the first round, you successfully hit the green in sub-regulation once and, on the second round, you successfully hit the green in sub-regulation twice. Your Sub-Regulation Accuracy *per Round* for the two rounds is 1.50.

**What does the Sub-Regulation Accuracy per Round stat tell us**

Knowing how often a player hits the green in sub-regulation shows how well they are driving the ball off the tee and how effective they are with longer clubs for their second shot. Generally speaking, a player may occasionally be able to drive a Par 4. On a Par 5, they will need to be on the fairway or have a good lie in the semi-rough to be able to hit the green. For example, if you are regularly going for a green in sub-regulation and missing, the following might be issues to consider:

- Course management. Is the appropriate club being hit off the tee to allow you to hit the green in sub-regulation?

- Do you have the correct clubs in your bag? It is possible you have too many wedges and not enough longer clubs to enable you to go for the green fully. It may be better for you to have an extra fairway wood or rescue club in the bag rather than one of those wedges.

- There may be a club defect with your longer fairway clubs

- Swing fault

- Not knowing how far they actually hit each club - misconceptions

# Stats form the foundation of our four building blocks that lead to better golf shots

The pyramid to success illustration, below, shows how keeping and correctly understanding stats forms the foundation for implementing correct swing changes. In this book, we are only dealing with the full swing although a stats report may highlight additional areas that require improvement. Assuming it's a full swing issue identified in the stats analysis, we now have the detail as to where we should be spending our time and energy. From here, you need to learn to understand the exact ball flight that is causing your game error. You are then going to learn exactly what has happened – at impact – to cause this shot and utilise the ideal swing references to build a powerful, consistent golf swing.

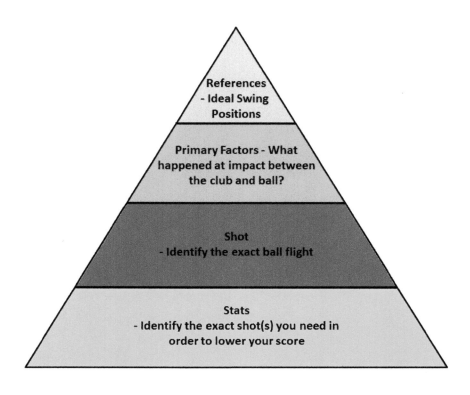

The illustration, above, examines the process to find the 'first point of failure'. The illustration below, on the other hand, helps find the point of failure for faults that aren't strictly due to swing technique. By looking at the data and then asking specific questions, explicit areas of improvement can be derived.

Continuing to record and monitoring your stats will indicate your improvements and help to build confidence.

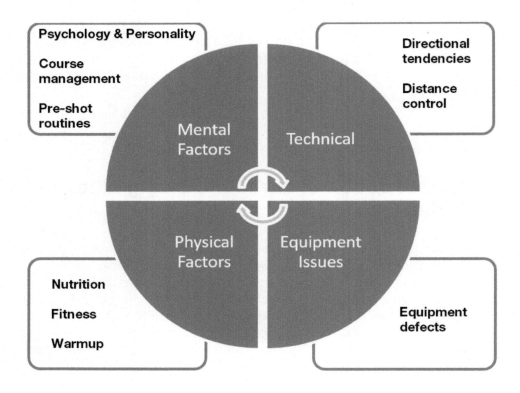

# Appendix

Example of a stats recording sheet from www.Strokeaverage.com (available on their website).

# Chapter 2
# Shot

Consistently getting the ball to do exactly what you want it to do, and land where it is intended, is a skill that can be developed. A good shot is a great contributor to a good round.

To be a skilled golfer, we need to understand not just how the ball will fly, but how the golf club influences the shot too. By which I mean, how the club face makes contact with the ball at impact and directly influences the quality of the strike, curvature, and flight.

As a golfer, we need to be able to deliver the club to the ball in a way that achieves our desired shot. This might be a straight shot or one that curves to the left, right, flies higher or lower. For the golfer looking to improve, I believe it is essential to have a clear and factual understanding of the impact laws that determine the ball's flight. This will help you deliver the club head in the desired way for your chosen shot and will also influence how you move your body and swing the club.

## Getting started

Let's begin with the 13 possible shapes of shot that can be produced when we hit a ball. Many people think there are hundreds of variations, but there are just 13.

When we are on our own and trying to fix our golf swing, the first thing we need to do is correctly diagnose the poor ball flight that we are consistently hitting. This sounds obvious, but please take a little time to really understand your main 'bad shape' of shot. If you keep stats, as previously recommended, this will be straightforward to identify. It's easy to get frustrated when not playing well and come to the conclusion that all of our shots are rubbish and they're going everywhere!

If a player doesn't have stats to show me, I will typically ask them (at the start of a lesson) to tell me about their contact with the ball: what direction are your poor shots starting and how are they curving? Often, the answer is "everywhere". At the next lesson, when I ask that question again, as I always will, I get a far more specific and factual answer. This is because my golfers have begun to understand that there will always be a pattern to ball flights. They may have two poor flights or strike patterns but not dozens. We are looking for the common destructive shot. From here, we translate what's happening between the club and ball during impact, then apply the right fix.

## Shot shapes

Below are the 13 shot shapes. This is the first point you need to understand before you can begin to fix your swing. It's important to understand that all of the flights are relevant to a player's intended starting and finishing target.

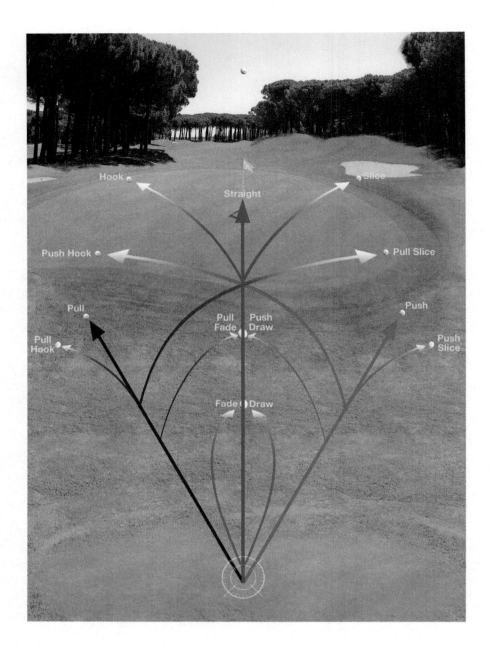

Firstly, we need to understand that spin is what creates the flight of the ball. From here we need to understand exactly how to control it.

Every shot will have a starting point to its flight and a finish point. During this, the ball may curve left or right and fly higher or lower than normal or expected. The best players in the world have the ability to control this flight at will. You can learn this.

The ball only ever spins on one axis. To become better golfers and to achieve a lower score we need to understand what causes the spin that leads to particular flight characteristics and then how we can control and manipulate it. The images below explain how a ball flies.

Imagine a golf ball suspended in mid-air, with a piece of string running horizontally through the center of it. If this ball rotates backwards, we would simply have backspin. We must have backspin in order to create lift and get the ball into the air. Assuming there is no wind, a ball spinning only backwards would produce a shot where the ball would fly in a straight line.

If we tilt this axis (the piece of string) left, it will curve the ball flight to the left. And if we tilt it to the right, it will curve it to the right.

The shot struck with a straight axis (e.g. the string is now horizontal/parallel to the ground) would see the ball start in a given forward direction and climb into the sky. The dimples on the ball help create lift force, up to two/three times more lift force than one without. A ball without dimples would still get some lift force. As the ball loses speed, it will fall straight out of the sky. The shape of flight will be straight; this could be straight towards the target, a pull or a push. Again this is assuming no external factors like wind. Below you can see an example using an airplane.

The red cross highlights the spin axis on a ball, and we can see that if this tilts left or right – just like a plane tilting its wings – the ball will change its direction of flight.

The amount we tilt the spin axis (string) left or right determines how much the ball will curve left or right during its flight. Additionally, the amount of spin also plays a key role in determining the amount of curvature. The higher the amount of spin the greater the curvature. The old terminology of side spin to describe a ball curving left or right is misleading. In this book, we will refer to it as *spin axis tilt,* and I would encourage you to think of it as spin axis tilt from now on.

The amount of spin a golf ball has will affect distance, height, and curvature. The most accurate way to measure the amount of spin is on a radar unit like TrackMan.

Okay, now we understand spin, let's move on to Primary Factors!

# Chapter 3
# Primary Factors

If we want to score lower, we need to understand and learn to control the collision between the club and ball. This collision is what will directly affect the strike and spin axis and flight of the ball. To hit any shot we desire, all we need to do is apply the club face to the ball in a certain way.

(All the references made below assume a right-handed golfer.)

Primary factors directly influence the shape and quality of the strike during the collision between club face and ball. They are:

1. Face angle
2. Club path
3. Attack angle
4. Dynamic loft
5. Smash factor
6. Impact location (highly related to point 5)

## Face angle

Face angle simply refers to the direction that the club face is pointing at the moment of impact relative to the target line. We must remember that the golf ball is on the club face for less than 1/2000th of a second. The exact point of the collision that will have the greatest influence on the direction of the ball is the mid-point of the collision (the point of maximum compression).

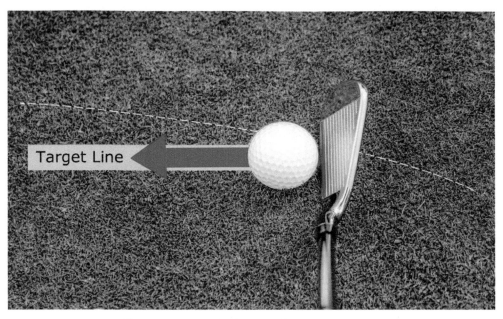

**Face angle relative to the target line.**

In general, the face angle has four times more influence on the start direction of the golf ball than the club path does.

# Club path

Club path is the horizontal direction that the club head is travelling during the collision. The part of the club head that a TrackMan radar will measure here is the centre of gravity of the club head.

Imagine a chalk line running along the ground from behind the ball, through the centre of the ball, and straight towards the target (we'll call this the target line). We refer to the club's path at impact as either swinging towards the target (i.e. straight down this line), swinging from inside to out, or outside to inside, of this line.

With a TrackMan radar, we can accurately measure the direction the club head is travelling in degrees through this impact zone. For example, and as a very general rule of thumb, if we want to hit a straight shot, the club path will be neutral (swinging along the chalk target line) through impact, with the club face pointing *at the target*.

A 'classic method' for hitting a draw (curving from right to left, for a right-handed player), on the other hand, would see the path being from inside the line on the ground to outside. For a fade (curving from left to right, for a right-handed player), it would be from the outside of the line to inside. For both the fade and draw, the face will be pointing midway between the path line and target line.

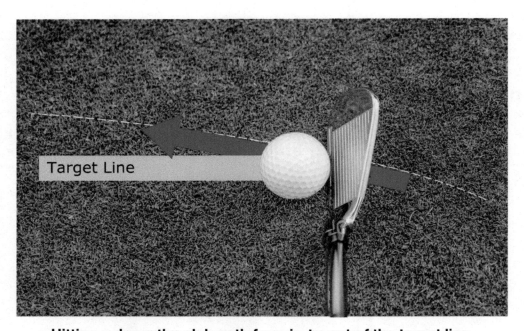

**Hitting a draw; the club path from in-to-out of the target line.**

# Attack angle

Your club's attack angle is the vertical angle at which the club head hits the ball. This, once again, is best measured in degrees.

With an iron or wood off the fairway, we should be looking for a downward angle of attack. For a wood off a tee, a slight upward strike is preferable.

**A downward strike that we would like to achieve with an iron.**

In general, the steeper the downward angle of the club head on the ball, the greater the spin will be. Hitting up on a driver (versus down) will help add distance.

It is generally accepted that the longest drivers of the ball have a more upward strike to their woods off the tee. Our shorter irons will typically have the steepest angle of attack, and this will reduce incrementally as the clubs get longer.

The images, below, illustrate two clubs just prior to impact. You can see that the more we hit down on the ball, the more the club head's path moves from in-to-out. The driver shows how hitting up on the ball creates a path that would be more out-to-in.

25

The following chart offers data that shows how distance is affected when we hit down, horizontally, and up on the ball with a driver. The chart shows the distance potential for a given club speed and angle of attack combination. If you hit up on the ball, you need less loft to launch the ball.

| Club Speed (mph) | Attack Angle (deg) | Ball Speed (mph) | Launch Angle (deg) | Spin Rate (rpm) | Carry (yards) | Total (yards) | Dynamic Loft (deg) |
|---|---|---|---|---|---|---|---|
| | -5 | 107 | 11.8 | 3214 | 140 | 182 | 14.9 |
| 75 | 0 | 109 | 13.0 | 2506 | 147 | 195 | 15.3 |
| | 5 | 111 | 15.3 | 1976 | 156 | 206 | 17.1 |
| | -5 | 115 | 10.1 | 3078 | 154 | 188 | 12.8 |
| 80 | 0 | 117 | 12.1 | 2494 | 163 | 199 | 14.3 |
| | 5 | 118 | 14.8 | 2005 | 174 | 209 | 16.5 |
| | -5 | 123 | 9.3 | 3110 | 169 | 215 | 11.9 |
| 85 | 0 | 125 | 11.7 | 2568 | 180 | 228 | 13.8 |
| | 5 | 126 | 14.0 | 1964 | 189 | 241 | 15.6 |
| | -5 | 131 | 8.5 | 3122 | 185 | 231 | 11.0 |
| 90 | 0 | 132 | 10.8 | 2517 | 196 | 245 | 12.8 |
| | 5 | 134 | 13.8 | 2021 | 207 | 259 | 15.3 |
| | -5 | 138 | 7.9 | 3144 | 201 | 247 | 10.2 |
| 95 | 0 | 140 | 10.5 | 2565 | 213 | 262 | 12.3 |
| | 5 | 141 | 13.0 | 1948 | 223 | 276 | 14.4 |

**TRACKMAN** — **Driver Fitting Chart: TOTAL Optimizer**

**Driver Fitting Chart. Image courtesy of TrackMan.**

# Dynamic Loft

**The dynamic loft of an iron at impact.**

Dynamic loft is the amount of loft the club face has at the moment of impact. This isn't necessarily the same as the 'measured loft' that a manufacturer gives a club. The main reasons for any difference are that, at impact, we may have shaft bend, shaft forward lean, the club face might be open or closed, the ball is struck on different parts of the club face, and the golfer's release of the club through impact is idiosyncratic.

## Smash factor

**The importance of a ball being struck in the centre of the club face.**

*'Technically, the smash factor says a lot about the centeredness of impact and the solidity of the shot – there is a strong correlation between the degree of centeredness at impact and the obtained smash factor'* – TrackMan

Smash Factor is a phrase used in the golf industry to describe the efficiency a golfer has when transferring club head speed into ball speed. It is the ratio between ball speed and club head speed. It is often discussed when players are trying to achieve the maximum distance they can.

Measuring ball speed with a radar is relatively straightforward. Club head speed is slightly more complex. When considering club head speed, we need to understand that there will be a difference in a club head's speed measurement depending on where we take the measurement from. There can be up to a 14% difference in club head speed between the heel and the toe of the club, the toe being the fastest.

With a driver, we're aiming to achieve the highest ball speed possible to get the ball the furthest distance we can. If a player has a high club head speed, that doesn't guarantee they will hit the ball great distances, unless it can be transferred to create a high ball speed. This transfer is very efficiently done when a player hits the ball from the centre of the club head.

As an example, with a driver, if a player with a club head speed of 100mph (average for a single figure golfer) were to hit the ball ¾ of an inch off-centre (towards the heel), they would lose about 5.5 mph ball speed compared to if they hit the centre of the club head. This loss of ball speed would lose them up to 10 yards. As a guide, we may lose up to 2 yards for each mph of ball speed lost.

You may have noticed that you get your longest shots when you hit the ball slightly higher on the face and towards the toe. This is because of the increased club head speed, slightly higher launch angle, and slightly lower spin rate that can happen from this part of the club head.

# Impact location

**A golf ball's impact location has a huge influence on ball flight.**

It is crucial to note the importance of hitting the ball from the centre of the club face. If this isn't understood and measured correctly, it is easy for a player or coach to come to the wrong conclusion about other primary factors.

A centred strike, in my opinion, is not spoken about or measured enough in coaching. The reason I put so much value on it, is the huge effect it has on both distance and direction. A simple way to see a strike pattern is to either use impact tape or a spray. I would use a foot spray that is used to treat athlete's foot. You can purchase it from most chemists. Simply spray a small amount across the face of the club. It will leave a very thin layer of powder that will clearly show, after you've hit a ball, where on the face the contact occurred.

For a driver or fairway wood, the effect of off-centre strikes for direction and shot shape are massive, especially with a driver. You may have noticed that the face of your woods has a slight curve from both top-to-bottom and side-to-side. This is referred to as the roll and bulge. The face is designed this way to try and correct for any off-centre strikes. Roll is the curvature from top-to-bottom on the face; bulge is the curvature from side-to-side on the face. The effect of roll and bulge with the ball is known as the gear effect.

## *How bulge works (for a right-handed golfer)*

Let's use a toe strike as an example. Firstly, because of bulge, the toe section is already pointing slightly to the right of the target. Secondly, if you hit the ball off the toe of the club, the collision will push the toe slightly backwards, slightly opening the club face to the target. This is because the toe, effectively, gets stopped momentarily by the ball but the heel keeps moving, opening the club face and starting the ball slightly to the right of the target. However, because of the gear effect, the ball will begin to spin in the opposite direction (left).

**A centred strike creates no twisting (open or closed off the face) and there is no gear effect.**

**A toe strike will twist the club face open and the gear effect will create a right to left spin axis.**

**A heel strike will close the club face and the gear effect will create a left to right spin axis.**

Vertical curvature (roll) from top-to-bottom of the club face has the greatest effect with regards to loft. As you can see from the image below, the top of the club is, in effect, sloping backwards in relation to the centre of the face, whereas the bottom of the club face is angled slightly the other way.

The loft, written on your driver, is normally a measurement from the centre point of the face. If you were to take a loft measurement from the top half of the face, it could be as much as 1.5º more than the middle. Conversely, if you were to measure the loft at the bottom of the face, it can also be as much as 1.5º less than the middle. In total, you would have a 3º difference between the top of the face and the bottom of the face.

What effect might this difference in loft have on your shots? When you hit a shot off the top part of the face, it will be similar to the heel and toe strike, causing the top of the club to slow down compared to the bottom of the club. Due to the same type of gear effect as we see with bulge, it will launch the ball higher and create less backspin.

Many people find that if they strike the ball slightly north of centre on their driver, they hit their longest shots. This is because they are launching the ball higher and with less spin. This will produce a shot that carries the ball further through the air. A shot struck from the bottom of the face will launch lower, with more backspin, making the ball's flight shorter. Again, you can see how the gear effect helps the golfer.

**The 'roll' curvature on a wood.**

**A ball being struck low on the face of a wood will reduce the
loft and increase the amount of backspin.**

## Swing direction

A secondary influence that is measured by TrackMan is swing direction. I have not included this in the primary influences as it's not part of the actual collision. However, you are most likely reading this book because you wish to improve and in order to do this, it's a critical factor for you to understand.

Swing direction has a link to club path. The best image I can give here is using the plane board.

During downswing, impact, and follow-through, imagine the club head swinging on top of this angled board. If the bottom edge of the board is placed on the ground and runs along my target line, it will give me a neutral/square swing direction. If it's turned to the right, so the bottom edge is now pointing to the right of the ball to the target line – that will give me an in-to-out swing direction.

If it's turned in the opposite direction – to the left and pointing left of the ball to target line – that would give me an out-to-in swing direction.

Swing direction is similar to the club path. The difference being the club path measurement is affected by *where* (during the swing), you make contact with the ball.

The three following images show the club just prior to impact, at impact, and just post impact.

If we look at points A, B, and C, the club is moving in three different directions relative to the baseline of the swing direction (the board). A to the right of the baseline, B parallel to the baseline, and C left of the baseline.

**Where we make contact with the ball, during the swing, has a direct consequence on the club path.**

Now I'm not suggesting you would ever hit the ball as early or late as points A and C illustrate, but they do illustrate (in a rather extreme way) how your club's path would be way right (in-to-out) or left (out-to-in), if you were to make contact at either of these points, although your swing direction hasn't altered.

To hit our desired shot, we need to get the correct club path at *impact*. Because we are likely to be hitting either up or down on the ball, we'll need to turn our swing direction to point in the correct direction (to get the club path where it needs to be for our desired shot).

Now you understand both the Primary Factors and Shots, let's have a look at the relationship between the two. Each of the shot shapes, given in Chapter 2, were labelled in the diagram. Below, you can see how the face angle relative to the target line, and the face angle relative to the club path, create each shot shape.

| Shot shape | Face angle relative to target | Face angle relative to club path |
| --- | --- | --- |
| Straight | Square | Square |
| Fade | Closed | Open |
| Pull Fade | Closed | Open |
| Slice | Square | Open |
| Pull Slice | Closed | Open |
| Push Slice | Open | Open |
| Push | Open | Square |
| Pull | Closed | Square |
| Pull Hook | Closed | Closed |
| Push Hook | Open | Closed |
| Hook | Square | Closed |
| Push Draw | Open | Closed |
| Draw | Open | Closed |

# Face to path

Face to path refers to the relationship between the face angle and the club path at impact. Assuming a centred strike, if the face is closed to the path, the ball will curve left. If the face is open to the path, it will curve right. The two key primary factors we need to get right for the desired shot shape are club path and face angle. If you can get these two correct, the ball will fly as (or very close to) how you intend it (assuming it is struck from the centre of the face and there isn't a wind influence).

There is an old saying relating to putting curve on the ball, "Path starts it, face bends it." This saying has arisen out of a lack of knowledge and is wrong. What we now know is that, for a wood, the club face accounts for approximately 85% of the ball's starting direction and approximately 75% with an iron. Any curvature will be as a result of the club head moving either to the right or left of the face angle during the collision.

Trying to hit a straight golf shot with poor technique can often feel like playing the national lottery. Every shot is taken with the hope that everything manages to combine effectively to give the desired result but often results in a less-than-perfect shot.

In golfing terms, a player is looking to match up their club face angle to their club path with a centred face strike. If any one of these factors is wrong, another factor also has to be wrong to compensate. You can be slightly out without too much effect, obviously, but more than a few degrees and you may have problems.

Imagine you're trying to hit a straight shot with a way open club face (pointing right). To get the ball to finish somewhere in the desired direction, one's instinct might be to have a swing direction that is way out-to-in, a club path that is left of the target line, and also a strike that is slightly off the toe. Now one thing to remember, this will all be happening subconsciously. Your behaviours adjust to your experiences; having adopted a particular technique, you will perpetuate it, and live with the 'hope' that the ball will go in the right direction.

My experience, over the years, has told me that golfers of all standards are pretty good at finding ways to get the ball into the air and which finish somewhere towards the target. This doesn't mean the ball will fly straight towards the target, get particularly high in the air, or (unfortunately) do anything consistently! But, occasionally, a golfer will hit a good shot by getting all their faults to cancel each other out. Even a broken clock tells the right time twice a day! The trouble – in golfing terms – is that we need our clock to tell the time far more often than twice a round! The rare good shot is where you've managed to match your faults all up. If you are the type of golfer who has two or three faults to try and match up on each shot, it gets much harder to play consistent golf.

Sometimes you'll get them matched up correctly for a few shots – the broken clock scenario. When you don't, disaster! That's when you hit your shots out of bounds with big hooks, slices, or top, and hit your shots fat. It is also when you become frustrated, and your emotional response feeds into your approach to the next shot.

Ultimately, to achieve your target of lower scores, consistency is the key.

# Chapter 4
# Swing References

Every golfer has his or her unique swing which they aim to perfect to achieve consistency.

This chapter will give reference to how I like to see a golfer swing and what I regard as ideal and neutral positions for good function during the swing. I'm not saying for one moment that if you don't swing it exactly as I describe you can't play good golf, simply these are my ideal references; positions I would encourage people to work towards.

When a player swings it close to these references, I don't see them needing to add in compensations. As I've said earlier, players can hit good shots by matching up their mistakes but having to rely on matching them up for each shot leads to inconsistency.

I always invest a lot of time working on the address position and as you will see it's the longest part of this chapter. But it is worth investing the time and effort here. If I help someone build a good setup, they are far more likely to swing correctly and hit better golf shots than if they have a poor set up.

Often, at the start of a lesson, I hear golfers say things like, "I've got this flying right elbow at the top of my swing I need to fix." These people have spent too much time trying drills, like having head covers under their right arm. This flying elbow is most often just a compensation for another fault earlier in the swing.

What we have to do is trace faults back to their origins, it's a lot like tracing a family tree. I can see your right elbow is disconnected from your body and 'flying'... but *why*?

When we trace things back to their origins, most often they start at address. In my experience, I honestly find that *most* swing faults originate at address. If you don't deal with the cause of the fault and only look at the one further down the line, it's likely you'll get little to no consistent improvement. We must identify the first point of failure. There may be three or more faults all linked together but we need to understand and begin at this first point of failure.

The very fact that you're reading this book tells me you want to get better and almost certainly you're willing to practice. It is worth noting that many people swing in a certain way based on what they *believe* to be correct; their preconceived concepts of what a correct swing should be. Someone may say, "Jim Furyk doesn't swing it as you describe." Sure, he doesn't, and I wouldn't for one second dream of asking him to. He has his style and one that has proven to be very successful. However, most golfers haven't developed a swing as productive as his. To me, Furyk has a few compensating factors throughout his swing but through years of practice and playing, he understands how to manage and consistently match them up, to return the club correctly at impact.

As a golfer looking to get better, we don't necessarily need to take the whole swing apart and rebuild it from scratch; just find the original swing faults that are contributing to the problematic shots that hold our golf back.

Some of the references described in this chapter have been done using the 3D data provided by friend and golf bio-mechanist, Mark Bull. Mark has worked with some of the best players in the world. The values supplied by Mark are for some segment rotations and positions, for example pelvis rotation, pelvis sway, etc. He and I have worked closely with players I have coached for many years. Mark uses his own 3D motion capture technology which he has developed. This allows us to accurately measure and quantify, in real time, how the body (joints and body segments) move. It is important to acknowledge Mark's involvement in this book has been to purely supply the numerical 3D values for some of the movements I am describing, as well as support and guidance as and when required. Mark has had no direct involvement in the written text.

Motion capture provides numerical values on areas such as joint range, segment control, and segment accelerations/sequences. It allows us to understand precisely how the golfer is moving during the swing. It also provides learning/stimulation devices such as real time biofeedback (audible tone) which provides a player with information when attempting to improve the behaviour of a selected segment, (e.g. pelvis rotation). Using a 3D system also provides objective, evidence-based measurement on how a player is moving during their swing. Having data on the player allows for more informed questions and assists us in understanding what areas need adjustment to achieve gains in performance, avoidance of pain, and development based on individual player priorities.

Motion capture allows the player to feel and understand, in real time, when segments move in the way they want, as well as what they are attempting to avoid. We must be aware that we are all human and built differently, and that past injuries may affect the way in which we are able to swing the club. Most golfers are likely to have anatomical imbalances and restrictions that will affect their ability to swing in certain ways. If a player does have an issue, they will most likely have found a way around it to enable them to hit the ball. Sometimes these issues can be fixed with the help of professionals, like physiotherapists, but sometimes we simply have to work around the issue. Understanding this fault process means that if there is a certain movement a player makes, due to physical limitation, we can correctly make an allowance in another area to balance it out and still allow the club to be delivered to the ball as desired.

**3D motion capture has given us the biomechanical knowledge of how to use our bodies most effectively and efficiently in the golf swing.**

All 3D references in this chapter assume a right-handed golfer using, unless otherwise stated, a standard length 6 iron based around the mean average length for the majority of manufacturers. The data is from a sample of over 100 golfers, both male and female with handicaps ranging from between 0 and 24. I acknowledge that there can be substantial variation in the data but for the purpose of the book, I've taken a mean average. It is important to allow for variability of movement through environmental and task change as well as anatomical constraints and conceptual understanding. By this, I mean a player may swing differently if the lie isn't flat, certain wind conditions are prevalent, or if they are looking to hit a shot shape other than straight.

At this early stage, I'd like to share with you a diagram of how the 'golfing body' should ideally function.

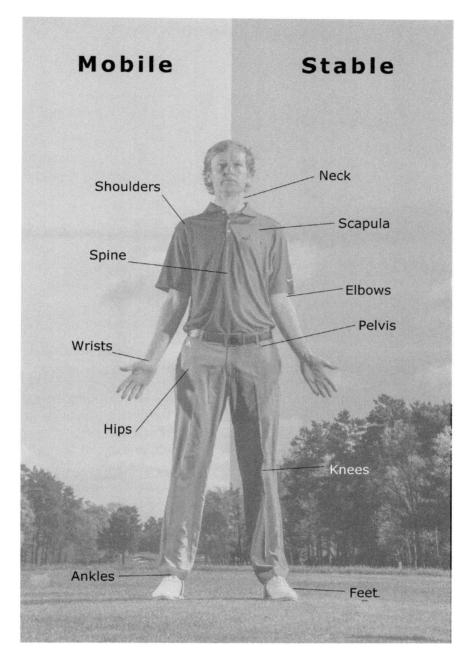

**The segments of the body that we'd like to be either 'mobile' or 'stable' during the golf swing.**

I was first introduced to a diagram like this by the Titleist Performance Institute. It simply demonstrates what we need to be stable, and what we need to be mobile, during the swing. It is a great image to have in your mind for understanding how certain areas of the body should function. Essentially, they are either mobile and moving, or stable and supporting.

As you read through this chapter, you will see I have broken the swing into references. We start at reference 1, the address position, before moving through to reference 9, the finish position. Within each reference I have, for simplicity, highlighted my four key areas:

- Club (handle, shaft, and club head)
- Hands and arms
- Lower body (feet, knees, and pelvis)
- Upper body (thorax and head)

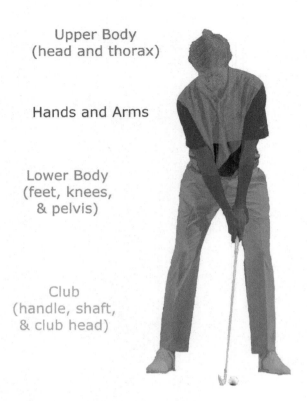

Upper Body
(head and thorax)

Hands and Arms

Lower Body
(feet, knees,
& pelvis)

Club
(handle, shaft,
& club head)

By breaking it down in this way, things will be easier to follow and practice. In each section, I have highlighted what I believe are the key points to check. I believe that it's called a golf swing because we are swinging the club and therefore it's a continuous, free-flowing movement. I wouldn't want you to get tense and rigid because of these references. Simply think of the references as places you're going to pass closely through during the swing.

Another reason I have broken the swing down into these segments is that they represent the correct kinematic sequence. The kinematic sequence is the order that the segments move and achieve their peak angular speed in the swing. It's fair to say that almost all highly-skilled golfers have a downswing kinematic sequence that would read: 1. Lower body > 2. Upper body > 3. Hands and arms > 4. Club Head.

But before we begin looking at the references, I'd like to discuss an often overlooked area that contributes to timing and rhythm issues. Getting your club and the main parts of your body all moving in time and correctly in sync.

The best analogy I can give to describe this, is the wheel of a car. Imagine the middle cap, where the manufacturer's logo resides and a small point at the bottom of this cap. Then, a small point, at the bottom of one of the car's tyres. When the wheel completes a turn, both these points will move 360° and arrive back at their starting point at the same time. The point on the tyre, however, has a far greater distance to travel to complete this full turn. Therefore the point on the tyre must move quicker to travel further and arrive at the same time as the point on the middle cap.

The golf swing works in a very similar way. If you imagine four points – the club head, hands, left shoulder, and left hip bone – moving from the address position to the top of the backswing, we want all four to move at their own correct speed, so as to arrive at the top of the backswing at the correct time.

The club head has the furthest to travel (it is not possible to provide an exact reference for this distance due to the significant number of variables involved). In turn, the hands travel about 65 inches (allowing for anthropometrical differences), the left shoulder about 10 inches, and the left hip about 5 inches. Therefore each will have to move at a different speed from the start of the swing to arrive at the top of the backswing at the same time. As an example, the segments could each achieve the following peak speeds in the backswing, club head ~600 d/s, lead hand ~400 d/s, thorax ~190 d/s, and the pelvis ~90 d/s.

**The club head, hands, thorax and pelvis
all correctly in sync in the backswing.**

Rhythm and timing are very important in 'gluing' the swing together. Candidly, I found the best way to understand and practice timing was from John Novosel's book and mobile phone App (Tour Tempo). He discovered, using a specific mathematical ratio, that the Tour pros he studied all had a similarity between the elapsed time their backswings took, and the elapsed time of their downswing. His research concluded for the full swing that the best players have a ratio of 3 parts backswing to 1 part downswing. The ratios don't all have to have to be the same, this is a personal thing. John concludes that all golfers, not just tour professionals, should have a ratio of either 18/6, 21/7, 24/8 or 27/9. Using the app, you can listen to the choice of four swing beats and then practice with the one that best suits you to give you a consistent swing rhythm.

# Reference 1 – Address

This first section to the chapter is crucial, like the foundations to a house. Get this right and you have something stable to build upon. Get it wrong and you are vulnerable to things going awry later in the swing. Rarely do I see a very good golfer with a really poor address position (and vice versa, a very poor golfer with a great address position). If you have a good setup, then you are far less likely to have other faults later in the swing.

As I have mentioned before, with the compensating scenario, if you have one fault in your swing, you are likely to have put another in place, later on, to compensate. The more compensating factors you have, the harder it is to play a consistent game. Consistency in our game gives us confidence and leads us to be in a strong mental state and make fewer mistakes.

Too many people make mistakes at address that can be avoided. If we create a correct, neutral setup, then a correct swing is far easier to make and feels like it just falls into place. Please take some time to get your address position correct. Regardless of ability, I feel all golfers, barring a physical reason, should be able to make the correct setup.

## *Club and shaft*

The club must sit correctly in terms of lie and alignment. So often this gets overlooked when learning golf. The correct lie of the club isn't what many people believe it to be, where the sole of the club sits completely flat on the ground. By having the club sitting completely flat on the ground it is difficult to get the handle to sit correctly in the fingers of your left hand and therefore the left wrist won't sit correctly at address. From here it then becomes difficult for you to get the correct radial deviation through your wrist joints in the swing. In addition to this, because the shaft will bend slightly downwards on the downswing (due to the weight of the club head) it will also cause a toe deep divot. This, in turn, will open the face through impact.

Having the club sitting incorrectly can often cause postural issues at address. The toe should sit slightly off the ground. You should be able to push a small coin, like a 5 pence about 1/4 of an inch under the toe of the club at the address position. This may feel a little bit alien to you if you have not already adopted this, but persevering in getting this right will pay dividends.

**The club sitting correctly at reference 1.**

The bottom groove of the club face should sit at 90° to the 'ball to target' line. Most manufacturers paint one or two of the bottom grooves white to help with alignment. Remember, the club face is directly responsible for where the ball travels. Its position at address can also affect your swing direction.

If, at address, when you look down at the club face, it is aiming right or left of your intended target, my experience says people are often likely to subconsciously react to this. They therefore adjust their behaviour to take account of what they see. This could be by creating a swing direction that matches or opposes this face alignment. Essentially, an incorrectly aimed club face at address is highly likely to cause a ball flight that's off-line. Most players will see this off-line ball flight and adapt their swing, when all they actually had to do to correct the flight was be aware of the face at address.

Often, the direction the face points at address is the one a golfer swings the club through impact.

The easiest way I have found to create correct alignment is to stand 6 feet directly behind the ball looking at the target. From here, pick a small point, ideally the size of a 5 pence piece, 1 foot in front of the ball, directly down your target line. **(See Left)** It could be a distinct tiny patch of grass that stands out, or an old tee peg on the ground. The common mistake is to pick a point further than 1 foot in front of the ball. Then when you place the club on the ground, take great care to align the club face towards this small point. Getting this right is so important – it will have an effect on your feet and body alignment.

When using irons, the club shaft will lean slightly towards the target at address. When using the woods, the shaft should be vertical. This position is similar to what we are intending to replicate at impact. A good reference is to imagine (from face on) that if the shaft were extended it would eventually hit a point under the left armpit.

**The correct shaft position at reference 1 for an iron and wood.**

The main influence for this lean is ball position. As a general rule of thumb, the hands will sit opposite the inside of the left leg for all clubs. I'll explain ball position later in the chapter but with a driver the ball is closer to the left foot. From here, it effectively moves back in our stance as the clubs get shorter until our wedges appear centrally.

As mentioned, with a driver we are looking to hit up on the ball and as the clubs get shorter we want a more descending strike. The more the shaft leans forward, the more this will encourage a golfer to hit down on the ball, de-lofting the club face and getting compression between ball and turf – ideal for irons. As with the driver, the shaft will be almost vertical and encourage a slight upward strike. Think of this as the 90° rule. I always like to see the shaft, at impact, to be close to 90° to the angle of attack.

As an example, with a mid-iron we'll aim to have an angle of attack of about -4°. Therefore our shaft will be close to 90° to this line, or about 86° to the ground. With a driver we may be looking for an attack angle of about +1°. Therefore our shaft angle will still be close to 90° to this, or about 91° to the ground.

**An iron displaying the ideal 90° shaft angle to attack angle.**

Bertie Cordle from DST Golf has a great analogy for this. "If you were hitting a nail into a piece of wood, you'd ideally have the shaft of the hammer at 90° to the nail." This 90° relationship between the club shaft and the attack angle is needed to get compression between the ball and club head. Better players may de-loft their club at impact slightly more than described, creating even more compression.

When viewing the shaft angle at address from down the line because it is sitting slightly 'toe' up (as mentioned before) the handle will also point towards your belt strap.

At this point, I must stress that I like a player to place the club on the ground correctly as described above, before taking their completed grip. Too many people take their completed grip then place the club on the ground. This is far less likely to produce either the correct grip or club face alignment.

## *Hands and arms*

### Grip - left and right hand

There isn't an absolute blueprint for holding the club correctly but we should aim for a neutral position as much as possible. Holding the club correctly is crucial to playing good golf.

Some people will have slightly stronger holds, where one or both the hands are turned further to the right. Others will have a weaker hold, where one or both are positioned slightly further to the left. The key is that if we stray too far from neutral then we will most likely have to add in further compensations, later, during the swing.

I don't mind players being a little off-neutral, just not too far. In this case, the way in which we set our hands on the handle will ultimately affect the club face position at impact. Aim for the neutral position and, if required, slightly strengthen or weaken this position to personalise matters and allow the club face to be square at impact.

The position of your hands can also affect how your arms will hang and where the grip pressure is in your hands. If you have a strong or weak positioned grip, then your forearms will tend to rotate too far to the left or right. This, in turn, will mean that you are likely to have a poor upper arm and upper thorax connection. As we go through the book, you'll see why it is important to have this connection.

A strong or weak grip can be caused by the handle not being correctly placed across the fingers and palms. Holding the handle too much in the fingers or palms makes it difficult to provide grip pressure in the correct places. This, in turn, can cause issues with radial deviation (cocking the wrists correctly), tension flowing up the arms towards the shoulders, and maintaining a secure hold during the swing.

I have heard people saying that one hand is more involved or important during all or part of the swing but this is not a theory I agree with. Getting the hands to work together, and in harmony with each other, will lead to a level of control that will enhance your technique.

## Left hand

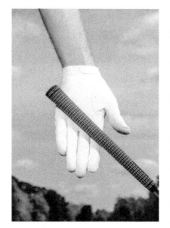

The first point when holding the club in your left hand is that I like to see about a 'two finger' gap between the end of the handle and the little finger. This will help ensure that your left hand sits securely on the handle and the fleshy pad doesn't creep off the top of it. Have you ever had a hole in this area of your glove? This hole is the club wearing against your glove as the handle slips during swing.

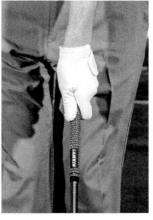

Firstly, place the club on the ground, lying correctly and aimed straight towards your target. With your hand flat, fingers straightened out and facing the ground, place the handle across your hand. The handle should run from the middle joint of the forefinger, diagonally across the palm, and exit between the base of the little finger and the bottom of the fleshy pad at the top of your palm. **(See Left for an example)**

From here, close your fingers around the handle. Then close your hand and bring the thumb over, so it sits just right of centre. **(See Right)**

If done correctly, the top part of the thumb and hand will be joined together and the end of the thumb will be level with the middle knuckle of the forefinger. This connection between thumb and hand will form a line commonly referred to as a 'V'. I like to see this 'V' point towards your right eye/ear. When looking straight down towards the hand, you should be able to see between 2 and 3 of your knuckles. **(See Left)**

An important point to understand here is that when you bring the thumb over onto the handle, allow the whole forearm, as required, to rotate over towards the right. If you only use your hand, you're likely to over-hinge your wrist and see 'cupping' in the wrist. The main hold/pressure should be in the last three fingers of the left hand.

I've heard many analogies over the years for this correct pressure level. For me it should simply be as light and tension-free as possible but one that will keep the club from sliding out of your hands. It may take practice but once you are confident about the right positioning, and it is consistent, it will become light and tension free.

## Right hand

The right hand can join with the left in one of three ways.

Baseball. This is where the right little finger sits on the handle next to the left forefinger. This is a good option for people with smaller hands or arthritic hand conditions.

Interlocking. This is also popular with people with smaller hands. Here the little finger of the right hand and the forefinger of the left entwine together.

The Vardon grip. Named after the record six-time Open Champion golfer Harry Vardon, it is the most common style and simply sees the right little finger sit in the gap between the left hand forefinger and middle finger.

With the handle correctly placed in the left hand, and your preferred choice of how the hands will join together, we need to look at how the handle will sit in the right hand.

We then need to apply the right hand. With your fingers pointing towards the ground place your right hand on to the side of the handle, so it runs from the middle knuckle of the forefinger, to the end knuckle of the little finger. The left thumb will sit opposite the lifeline of the right hand. From here join your hands together using your chosen method then wrap your fingers around the handle.

From here, place your right palm on top of the left thumb.

The left thumb should sit comfortably in the slight cavity in the right palm that is formed when placing the right hand on top.

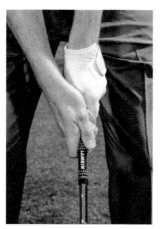

I like to see the right-hand thumb sit just over the left side of centre on the handle. The left thumb should be totally covered. A 'V' will again be formed between your right thumb and hand. I like this to sit parallel to the left hand's 'V'.

On the right hand, the middle knuckle of the forefinger should sit on the side of the handle in a 'trigger-like' position, so it can help to provide pressure onto the ball through impact. The end of your right thumb should sit level with the bottom of your right forefinger when the grip is complete. On the right hand, you will be able to see two of your knuckles when looking down in the address position. The main pressure points of the right hand are the middle two fingers. Again the amount of pressure is the same as the left hand.

Golfers are happy to invest in the right clubs but often a lack of consideration is given to ensuring that they have the correct handle size. This should not be neglected. The larger your hands, the larger your handle will need to be. Equally if you have small hands you may need smaller-than-standard size handle. As a guide I like to see the fingers of the left hand comfortably just touch the left palm when gripped correctly.

## *Lower body*

Starting from our feet, working up to our pelvis.

I measure the width of a player's stance in relation to the width that the left and right heels sit apart. I don't like to see a huge difference in width between all the clubs. The narrowest stance would be with wedges and that will get wider as the clubs get longer. The narrowest stance (used with the wedges) should see the inside of the heels under the armpits. The stance gradually gets wider, with the driver being the widest and the inside of the heels being towards the outside part of the shoulders. This ties in with ball position.

I teach a static ball position system. I like to see the ball positioned for all irons about 4 inches inside the left heel. This means, for wedges, it's near to the centre; the right foot moves out as the irons get longer (the ball position, relatively speaking, moves forward in the stance). With fairway woods and rescue clubs, I like the ball to be positioned 2 inches inside the heel and with a driver (off of a tee peg) 1 inch inside the heel.

**Wedge**                    **Mid-Iron**

**Rescue**　　　　　　　　　　　**Driver**

It's important to understand here that, with all the clubs with the ball placed on the ground, we are looking for a downward strike. The only time we want to be hitting up on the ball would be when playing a wood, off a tee peg. The more centred a ball position, the more it promotes a downward angle of attack.

How should the feet be positioned? I like both feet to be equally turned out. Conventionally, people have their right foot closer to 90 degrees to the target line and only the left foot turned out. The issue I have here is that this positioning creates an imbalance in how the hips function. The hips should be allowed to move freely and naturally in both the back and forward swing; an imbalance prevents this from occurring. Turning feet out by different degrees will only cause restrictions at some point during the swing. Ankle and feet positions have a significant influence on lower limb and lumbar spine/pelvis function. This also ultimately leads to stresses on your body if not done correctly.

Having the foot and ankle in a neutral position at set up will allow for the maximum range of motion through other joints, primarily the hip joint. This will allow for optimal pelvis movement which will consequently encourage the spine to move and rotate with minimal adaptation. Anatomically, having the feet externally rotated to approximately 20-30° allows each foot to point in the correct position thus allowing for good lower limb and hip joint function.

**Both feet correctly positioned to allow for the
correct rotation of the pelvis and thorax.**

Imagine, when taking your address position, a clock face for each foot, with 12 o'clock being directly in front of you. The left foot I like to see turned out pointing to 11 o'clock and the right foot turned out to face 1 o'clock. From here, I like the weight to be distributed evenly, for all clubs, 50% under each foot. The exact point is in the centre of the foot, just at the front of each ankle. This creates good balance and stability to swing the club from. This will change as we swing the club but only from a lateral point of view. I like a player to feel that the weight stays at the fronts of the ankles all the time during the swing. The only time this changes, is at a point where the right foot moves onto its toe during the follow-through.

Alignment. For a straight shot I like to see a players' feet parallel to the 'ball to target line'. A common mistake is that people tend to aim their feet directly at the target, which effectively means they're aiming right. Using your ball to target line as a baseline, if a line were placed along the front of your toes, I like this to be parallel to the ball to target line. This can be practiced, simply, by laying a club down on the ground at the front of the ball pointing at the target. Place a second club, two feet left of that club and parallel to it. From here, taking your address position, the front of both your feet should be parallel to this second club.

**The feet placed parallel, correctly,
to the ball to target line.**

Because of the way we set our pelvis and thorax at address, these two areas will be between parallel to the target line and a few degrees anti-clockwise (open). Generally, the pelvis is closer to parallel than the thorax. The pelvis can sit up to 5° open, whilst the thorax can be up to 5° to 8° open at address.

The knees should sit in a natural position. Neither pushed in or out uncomfortably. Generally, I see people with their knees pushed in more than I see them pushed out. A natural position will allow your hips to function correctly during the pivot. Ideally, I want your knees to sit under the corresponding hip socket. When the knees sit correctly, they will keep a player's weight in the middle of the feet, not putting pressure on the instep or outside of the feet. Good for your golf as well as your joints!

The amount of knee flex is also important. If you were to lock your knees so as to have straight legs, I'm then looking for you to simply un-lock them. You don't want to be sitting down. If, when set up and ready to hit a shot, you looked down at your feet – with the correct amount of knee flex – all of the fronts of your shoes will still be visible. A simple check is if you hold a cane on the front of your knee and drop it down towards your feet, it should touch the ball joint of your big toe.

The pelvis area is another crucial area that is simple to get correct but which often gets overlooked. This is a key part in getting balance correct in the feet. When looking at your setup from down the line, I would advise having your left and right greater trochanter (illustrated by the blue mark on the image below) sitting above each corresponding ankle. Looking down the line, you will notice your belt line tilting forward, indicating a pelvis forward bend of between 12° and 18°. This is crucial in getting the body into a position that will allow the spine to tilt forwards correctly. From face on, the centre of the pelvis (close to where you would have your belt buckle placed) will be centred between the feet. It's also important to appreciate that when you increase the side bend (lateral flexion) of the spine (we'll cover the upper body next), it may create a small anti-clockwise rotation through the thorax, This may then cause the pelvis to sit very slightly rotated anti clockwise (open) at reference 1.

The rear of your glutes, viewed from down the line, will be sitting behind your heels.

## Upper body

Ideally, you should tilt your thorax over from your hip joints. **(See Left)** Don't confuse this with the waist! This is referred to as flexion, however I shall refer to it as forward bend for the rest of the book. The amount of forward bend could be 35° to 45°.

It is acceptable for the thorax to be up to 8° open. Placing a club across your ribcage and shoulders for an accurate measure of this presents some challenges, primarily because we are looking at the alignment of the thorax at set up, not the shoulder joints as one of the shoulders/scapula could be excessively protracted. This would influence the direction the club is placed in, despite the thorax being neutrally aligned.

Your shoulder blades should remain relaxed (down) in the same way they would be if you were standing in a normal, correct upright posture. Commonly, I see people lifting their shoulders up and forwards at address. Your head should have maintained its position from the correct posture you had (stood upright before you began to lean over). I often see people with their chin dropping forwards and down rather than held in its correct position.

We all have a natural amount of curvature to our lower spine and we should let this sit comfortably in a natural way. Too often, I see people pushing their backside out/back too far and this increases curvature, which is unnecessary and uncomfortable.

The face should appear relaxed as the head is sitting naturally.

As the right hand sits lower than the left on the club, I look for the thorax to have a slight lateral flexion to the right. I shall refer to this lateral flexion as side bend for the rest of the book. This happens from a point at the very base of the spine, the tail bone, and stays constant to the back of the head and at an angle of between 6° to 9°. Make sure not to make this movement from the thoracic (middle) part of your spine. Despite this side bend, your weight remains equal under both feet.

You should aim for the majority of forward bend **(See Left)** and side bend **(See Right)** to remain during the swing until impact. This is because it will have a major influence on your swing direction through impact. Generally, if you have too much side bend to the right at address, or during the swing, the swing direction will work too far from the inside to the right. If you have too much side bend to the left, your swing direction is likely to be too far from the outside, slicing across the ball through impact.

**The correct side bend (lateral flexion).**

The arms should be hanging from the shoulders, tension free. As a reference, your left thumb will be at a point under your chin/neck area. I like to see the upper part of both arms connected to the rib cage area of the upper body. I'm not looking for tension, or pressure in this area, just a slight connection. Because of the side bend to the right from the thorax, the left arm will be comfortably straight but the right elbow will be slightly hinged. Because of this, the top of the left forearm will be just visible if viewed from down the line. Due to the position of the shaft and the upper body, the hands will appear – from face on – to be just inside the left thigh.

As you can see, all the above advice contributes to reducing the strain and tension in your body and therefore contributes to game improvement. It's also kinder to your body and if you want to continue to play golf for a long time you need to look after your body as well as improving technique.

# Reference 2

## *Club and shaft*

From down the line, the shaft will appear to be at the same angle that it was at address but moved slightly to the inside of the ball (closer to the body).

If you can... imagine a curved railway track. Viewed from directly above the golfer, the club head would appear to move away from the ball on the outer track whilst the hands would be on the inner track. At this reference we've simply moved our hands and club along the tracks. The butt of the club will still be pointing at our belt line and the club face has rotated slightly clockwise (open) but will still be square to the path. People sometimes make the mistake of moving the hands towards and onto the outer track. This, in turn, then causes the club head to move onto the inner track!

When doing a practice swing, I will often use a plane board to help a player feel the correct movement. It sits under the shaft of the club and encourages the player to swing the club back on the correct path and plane to reference 3. I'll also refer to it later again, in reference 8, to keep the club on plane.

**The plane board is a great tool for getting the club to swing back on the correct path.**

## Hands and arms

With your hands, grip pressure will be the same as at address.

## Wrist action

Due to significant variability, for the purpose of this text I will just define and explain the direction the wrists move through.

These illustrations show the functions each of the wrist will perform during the swing. The table gives an example of what anatomically-healthy wrist function may be for each wrist during the backswing, downswing and how they will be positioned at impact compared to address.

**Neutral Wrist**

**Supination**

**Pronation**

**Radial Deviation**

**Ulnar Deviation**

**Wrist Extension**          **Wrist Flexion**

|  | **Left Wrist** | **Right Wrist** |
|---|---|---|
| **Backswing** | Pronation | Supination then pronates |
|  | Radial deviation | Radial deviation |
|  | Flexion (could still be extended at the top of the backswing) | Extension |
| **Downswing** | Pronation | Supination |
|  | Ulnar deviation | Ulnar Deviation |
|  | Flexion | Extension |
| **Impact (compared to address position)** | moving into supination | moving into pronation |
|  | Ulnar deviation | Ulnar deviation |
|  | Flexion | Extension |

To me, the wrist function in the backswing is like the second hand of a clock. As the club begins to move, the wrists start to function all the way to the top of the backswing.

I acknowledge that there is significant variability achieved through the wrist due to the ranges the wrists achieve and move through; the influence of task and environment on club delivery alongside constraints placed on the player such as anatomical imbalances and swing/coaching preferences all have an effect. Therefore, although there are many exceptions to what has been described above, listed is what is considered healthy, anatomical and biomechanical wrist function.

Part of the upper arm will maintain its connection to the rib cage area of the upper body but the right elbow will begin to hinge (flexion). In response to good wrist function, this will allow the right humeral head/shoulder joint **(See Left)**, to sit down which will encourage lateral rotation around the shoulder whilst the scapula remains down (depressed). At this stage, your right arm elbow joint should not be moving backwards behind your body. The right elbow should stay in front of the right hip joint. This will ensure it maintains its connection with the thorax and help keep the hands and club in front of the body.

The left upper arm will, again – like the right – maintain its connection to the rib cage area of the upper body. Imagine, once more, the inner railway track. It would be located below your hands at address and your hands have simply moved along this track. If you look down at your hands you will see they appear just in front of your right toes. Because of this, the left arm will begin to adduct slightly, and move across the chest $< 10°$. This is also to do with the fact, as explained earlier, that the club and arms are both moving quicker than the thorax. The left arm will then start to pronate, rotate clockwise.

## Lower body

Your weight will have begun to shift over to the right foot but only slightly. Our right leg maintains its position, keeping its flexion, whilst the left knee has the freedom to begin moving laterally towards the right whilst still supporting the body above. The pelvis will have also started to rotate clockwise.

## Upper body

Here the thorax has also begun rotating clockwise. The player will have maintained the thorax side bend and forward bend from address. It is important, at this early stage, for the player to ensure that they have kept their shoulder blades down in the same place they were at address. A common fault is for the player to lift the right shoulder. The gap between the right shoulder and right ear should be the same as it was at address.

# Reference 3

## Club and shaft

At this stage, the shaft will have moved back to a point where it is now parallel to the ground. If your toe line that runs parallel to the target line were continued on the ground (running away from the target) the shaft will sit close to being on top of this line at this point. Again, the club face will be in a square position in relation to the path. To explain this, viewed from down the line, the face will appear to be slightly face down, almost at a parallel angle to the thorax.

## Hands and arms

From face on, the hands will appear on, or close to, the right shoe at this stage; and from down the line, the hands will be at the front of the toes as they continue to move along the correct path. The back of the left and right wrists should have maintained the formation/structure that they had at address.

The right elbow will have continued to hinge (move into flexion) but not elevate, whilst the upper part of the arm keeps its connection with the rib cage area. At this point, I would still like to see the right elbow joint in-front of the right hip. A simple way to make sure this happens is by ensuring it stays in front of the seam that runs up the side of the shirt. It's important to realise that the right elbow will also have an amount of rotation at this point.

The left arm will be comfortably straight and continue its connection with the thorax. Viewed from down the line, the left arm will now appear close to parallel to the toe line.

The left arm will have continued to pronate.

## Lower body

Here, your weight will have gradually continued to move further over the right foot whilst the right leg stays in position, again maintaining its flexion. The right femur will begin to turn slightly clockwise in response to the pelvis itself turning further clockwise. This is an important point. Although the right leg is stationary, because the pelvis is rotating, the upper leg will have movement. The left and right side of the pelvis will still appear to be level. The right glute will have maintained its position in relation to how far it sits behind the right heel. This is a common reference point for me. If a player keeps their glutes a similar distance behind their heels, and the front of their head a similar distance in front of their toes like they had at reference 1, I know they will maintain their thorax forward bend during the swing. This, like thorax side bend, is a crucial element in helping to have a correct, consistent swing direction. Commonly, players lose connection with one or both of these references, ultimately meaning their thorax will have moved upright.

## Upper body

The thorax will have continued to turn clockwise around its axis, keeping its forward bend and side bend. The head and neck will also still be relaxed and, if required, the head can have some rotation to the right. A mistake is to keep the head rigidly still. If it wants to, a little movement is okay and assists thorax rotation. Another focus should be the distance between right ear and right shoulder; it should be maintained. Again, this tells us the right shoulder blade is functioning correctly.

# Reference 4

## Club and shaft

At reference 4, I like to see the bottom grooves, or the leading edge of the club face, close to parallel to the ball to target line. This means that the face has remained in a square and neutral position. The shaft will bisect somewhere between just below the right shoulder and bicep area, whilst the butt of the club aims at a point behind the ball.

## Hands and arms

The right elbow will have continued to hinge but should allow the upper arm to have maintained some of its connection to the upper rib area (but less than in reference 3). The right elbow will appear opposite the seam of the shirt.

The left arm will have remained comfortably straight, slightly across the chest, just inside from being parallel to the toe line and parallel to the ground. From down the line, the hands should be almost opposite the sternum. From face on, the tops of both elbows will appear almost level. The left arm will have continued to pronate.

## Lower body

Here, the right foot will still be grounded and the weight will have continued to move across to the right foot. It would be at about this point that I would expect to see the maximum amount of weight transfer into the right foot.

A common mistake is for the pelvis to sway to the right because a player is trying to get their weight into the right foot by overusing the lower body. We feel the weight shift in our feet but it's not created from a sway of the pelvis. What creates the feeling of more weight in the right foot is the fact that the thorax has rotated around its axis and the hands, arms and club are now positioned to the right of the golfer's body.

The right knee will have maintained its flexion whist allowing the right thigh to have a little more rotation. Keeping the flex helps the pelvis to rotate on the correct axis and keep pressure in the correct part of the right foot. The left knee will have maintained its support for the pelvis but will continue to move slightly across to the right knee. The pelvis will have rotated approximately 30-35°

clockwise but the left and right side of the pelvis will have remained close to horizontal when viewed from face on. As in reference 3, the right glute will have maintained a very similar distance behind the right heel that it had at reference 1.

## Upper body

The thorax will have continued to rotate, moving approximately 60-70° clockwise. The head may have turned slightly further to the right but will have maintained a very similar height and position to what it had in reference 1. The thorax will have maintained forward bend and side bend. Both shoulder blades will have remained in the down position.

# Reference 5

## *Club and shaft*

Here the shaft will be short of parallel to the ground for our irons and work its way close to parallel for the driver. The shaft will point left of the target if viewed from down the line with irons and only point near to parallel to the target when the shaft has swung almost all the way round and reached close to parallel to the ground. To help explain this, imagine a hula hoop parallel to your target line, at a 45º angle off the ground and you are looking at it from down the line. If I were to place a pen flat on the perimeter of the hoop at reference 4 it would be clearly pointing left of the target. Only as I continue to slide the pen around the hoop will it get nearer to this… pointing parallel to the target line. In fact, only at the very top of the hoop would it point there.

**Varying lengths of swing, and the directions that the
shaft points as the swing length changes.**

If I was to be a player with an over swing, and there have been many successful players that have (e.g. John Daly) then the club should point to the right of the target at reference 5. Again, imagine the pen on the hoop and if I slide it beyond the top of the hoop it would start to point right of the target. At this point, a square club face is when the club face is close to being parallel to the left arm.

## Hands and arms

The back of the left wrist will again have maintained a similar structure to the one we saw at address. This helps to maintain a square club face position. The left arm – straight but relaxed – will have a fractionally steeper plane than our shoulder plane. Keeping the left arm straight helps to maintain width in the arc of the swing.

At this point, it would be clear to see how the left arm and the shoulder plane's relationship alters in the backswing (depending on the club we are using). As a guide, I would expect the left arm and shoulder plane to be a fraction steeper with shorter irons than it is for mid-irons, and a fraction flatter with longer clubs; at address, the shorter clubs will require a player to bend over more from the hip joints. This, in turn, increases the thorax bend for the player to rotate around, resulting in a steeper shoulder and left arm plane at the top of the backswing. The opposite would happen for longer than mid-irons. Because the longer shaft will have encouraged a more upright posture at address, the shoulder and left arm plane will be flatter at reference 5.

The right elbow will have hinged but the upper arm will still have maintained a fraction of its connection to the right side of the upper rib/arm pit (axilla) area. If, from down the line, you were to draw a line down the centre of the right forearm, I like to see this line sit between pointing at the rear glute area and being parallel to the spine.

The left arm will have continued to pronate. At this point, the dimple on the inside of the left elbow will point towards the right shoulder.

The hands will appear, from down the line, to be above the right bicep/shoulder area.

## Lower body

At this point, I would expect to see your weight beginning to transfer from the right foot into the left foot – creating traction from your feet, and the ground, to unwind from in the downswing.

The right knee will have maintained most of its flexion; however, it is likely that it will have moved fractionally towards extension. This is influenced by the direction the pelvis has moved in, and bone structure.

The left knee will have continued to move towards the right knee. At this point, it's worth noting that – for players who may have limited rotation in their body – the left heel may lift off the ground slightly to assist the turn.

Performed correctly at this point, I would expect to see the right leg at a very similar angle – from face on – to what it displayed at address. If anything, the right leg may appear to be angled a little more towards the target. This is due to how the pelvis turns, and its shape. The pelvis is wider than it is deep, so when we correctly turn around the centre of our pelvis it remains in the centre of our feet. This explains why the right leg would appear in this way.

From down the line, the left knee will now be partially visible.

The pelvis will have rotated to its maximum point, approximately 35-45° clockwise from reference 1. As a guide, this would show the belt buckle pointing close towards the right knee. From face on, the left and right side of the pelvis will still appear relatively level. From down the line, the forward bend of the pelvis will still be visible, showing the player has maintained their posture. As before, the right glute will still be positioned a similar distance behind the heels.

## Upper body

The thorax will have turned approximately 85-95° clockwise from reference 1. It will have maintained the majority of the forward bend and side bend that we created at address. Maintaining these angles is crucial to being able to create a correct swing plane.

Both shoulder blades should have remained down, as per address. The head will have stayed in its position, tension free but – if required – turned a little further to the right.

The body should be acting like a wound up spring, here, due to how the muscles function.

# Reference 6

## *Club and shaft*

At reference 6, I like the club face to (again) be very similar to reference 4. The butt of the club will be aiming at a point behind the ball. This tells me the shaft is on plane, ready to deliver the club head on the correct path into the ball.

Here the shaft will be on a similar plane to reference 4. It may be a fraction shallower, bisecting the right bicep.

## *Hands and arms*

The left arm will have maintained its structure and appear straight, and the upper part of the arm will be connected to the chest. The left arm will begin to supinate; the right arm will begin to pronate. If, in the backswing, it was winding up it is now unwinding. The right arm will still be hinged and the back of the right tricep will begin to reconnect to the right upper ribs. From face on, the elbows will appear close to level with each other, the right may be slightly below the left.

Because the club head has begun to increase its speed, grip pressure will have slightly increased. However, this isn't something we should try and do. It is a natural, subconscious reaction to the increase in speed and operates in anticipation of impact.

## *Lower body*

Your weight will have continued to transfer into the left foot. The left foot will be firmly planted onto the ground. The right shoe will still be planted on the ground but the right heel will, from here on, gradually lift off the ground.

The left leg will have maintained some of its flexion, marginally more than in reference 1 at this stage, and be braced to accommodate the transfer of weight. The right knee will be moving towards the left but will have maintained its flexion.

The pelvis will have swayed to the left by approximately 7-10 cm since reference 5. It will have started to turn anti-clockwise and unwind. As before, the left and right side of the pelvis will (from face on) appear level.

It is important to check, at this stage, that although the pelvis has rotated, the glutes are still behind the heels as per the previous positions, indicating that you have maintained the correct posture.

## Upper body

The thorax will have maintained forward bend and side bend from previous positions. It will have continued to turn anti-clockwise but would still be approximately 45-50° turned to the right/clockwise (in relation to square to where it would have been in reference 1).

I would also look for the head to be in a similar position to before.

# Reference 7 (Impact)

## *Club and shaft*

Here the club face will be 90° to the ball to target line for straight shots. The top section of the shaft will have moved fractionally more upright compared to address when seen from a down the line view (right hand image). Due to the way the head was positioned at address and combined with a slight downward bending from the shaft, the sole of the club head will have a level contact with the ground. This is all due to centrifugal forces from having a heavy club head on the end of a flexible shaft. It will, however, appear from down the line very close to where it was positioned at reference 1.

The shaft will also have a forward lean, meaning we will have de-lofted the face slightly. This de-lofting of the club face creates pressure on the ball between the face and ground. Bertie Cordle from DST Golf, refers to this as 'the line of tension'. He correctly explains this line of tension as a line from the centre of the left shoulder down to the golf ball. To get consistent control of the face and pressure between the club head and ball, the hands must be in front of this line.

**(Left: A powerful and controlled impact with the hands correctly in front of the 'line of tension'.)**

The low point of the club's swing arc will be several inches in front of the ball for a mid-iron and move back, as the clubs get longer, to a point at the back of the ball for a driver.

## Hands and arms

Grip pressure will be slightly greater at impact than at reference 1 due to the golfer anticipating impact and subconsciously ensuring the face is stable through impact, especially if a divot is being taken. This is a subconscious reaction and something that you shouldn't try to create.

The left arm will, from face on, appear comfortably straight. It will also have a similar upper arm connection to the one felt at reference 1.

The right arm will have a slight hinge but the upper part will have connection to the rib cage.

## Lower body

I would expect to see the majority of your weight now located in the left foot. I like to see the left foot still comfortably flat on the ground at this stage; however, this depends significantly on the individual's ankle and hip range. This is an indication of good balance and the player staying in their posture. The right foot will have rolled slightly onto the inside part of the foot and the right heel will be slightly off the ground.

The left knee will be in flexion, however it will be moving towards and into extension. From face on, it will appear vertical. I don't like to see any collapse towards the target here. The left hip, knee, and ankle will appear stacked on top of each other. The right knee will still be in flexion and continue to move across towards the left knee.

The pelvis will have continued to rotate and unwind anti-clockwise, it will now be turned approximately 30-40° anti-clockwise from its position at reference 1. The left side of the pelvis will be slightly higher than the right. The left glute will have maintained a similar position/distance behind the left heel that it had at reference 1.

## Upper body

At this point, the thorax will have rotated further anti-clockwise and now be rotated approximately 15-25° anti-clockwise from its position at reference 1. The amount of forward bend will be similar to what we had at reference 1, and side bend will be around 30°-40°.

The head will have dropped slightly, 2-6cm with a slight thrust, 2-5cm negative, away from the ball.

# Reference 8

## *Club and shaft*

At reference 8, the shaft will be just short of parallel to the ground. Using the shaft plane line (as in reference 2) as a reference, the shaft will appear to be running up and on this line. Again, like in reference 2, using the plane board demonstrates this well. This tells me the player's club head and hand path are correct.

**The club and shaft on plane with a controlled, square club face.**

Although working on the opposite side of the ball, the club face will be mirroring the orientation as mentioned in references 2, and will be square to the path.

## Hands and arms

The right hand may be feeling like it is moving slightly on top of the left.

The right arm will have straightened and the left will have begun to hinge but both will have maintained their upper arm connection to the upper ribs.

## Lower body

The weight will have continued to move further into the left foot. The right foot has continued to move off the ground, with the weight on the inside ball of the right foot. The right heel will have moved off the ground allowing the lower body to unwind.

The left leg will now be almost totally straight whilst the right knee has continued to move across towards the left knee. This means the right leg will still have some flex.

The pelvis will be rotated approximately 45-60° anti-clockwise from its position at reference 1, with the left hip bone still higher than the right.

## Upper body

The thorax will have kept its forward bend but only about half the amount we had at reference 7. Side bend will have increased by around 10° (away from the target) compared to reference 7. Both can be seen as the body starting to move into a more upright posture. The thorax will be approximately 40-55° rotated anti-clockwise from its reference 1 position. Viewed from down the line, the shoulder line will be in an almost parallel, mirrored, position to reference 3 due to the shoulder blades sitting correctly.

The head will be looking somewhere between the ground and the club head. Allowing the head to rotate encourages and allows the thorax to unwind. Essentially, the golfer's eyes are looking at and tracking the ball.

# Reference 9 Finish

## *Club and shaft*

The club head will have fully released here. From down the line most, if not all, of the grooves on the club face will be visible.

At this point, you should expect to see the shaft at a slight downward angle, parallel to the shoulder line, with the middle part of the shaft opposite the bottom of the head or neck line.

## *Hands and arms*

The hands will be above the left shoulder.

Both arms will be relaxed. The right arm will be across the chest whilst the left will be hinged. The left tricep/elbow joint will (from down the line) be above the left hip.

## *Lower body*

The left foot will have remained on the ground, but will have moved onto its lateral border. The right is now completely on its toe and all of its spikes out of the ground. The majority of weight will now be in the left foot.

The knees will have come together. The left leg will be, from both angles, comfortably straight. The right will be flexed.

The pelvis will have completely unwound now with the belt buckle looking towards the target. From down the line, the top of the pelvis will appear parallel to the ground. From face on, the pelvis will look as though it is stacked and sitting above the left leg.

## Upper body

From face on, the thorax will appear stacked and sitting on top of the pelvis. The thorax will have completely unwound with the sternum facing the target. There will be a slight side bend seen from down the line, and because of this the right shoulder will be slightly lower than the left. From face on, the head down to the left foot will appear to be in a straight line.

The head, when viewed from down the line, will match and follow a line running up the centre of the thorax to the top of the head.

I like a player to hold this finish position until the ball has reached at least the apex of its flight. This shows commitment to the shot and good poise and balance. I find holding this position also has a positive effect on the whole rhythm of the swing.

I have explained the above details assuming a player was practicing with a mid-iron. If a shorter club was being used, I would expect more forward bend in the posture at address and the club to be swung on a slightly more upright plane. Conversely, with a longer club, I would like to see a player stand with slightly less forward bend and the club swung a little more rounded. Both of these changes occur because of shaft length changes.

# Chapter 5
# Bringing it all Together

## How to use what you've now learnt most effectively

You now have excellent knowledge of my four key components for improving golf:

1. Statistics
2. Shot
3. Primary factors
4. Swing references


I'd now like to share with you some of my thoughts – along with performance coach Karl Morris – on how humans effectively learn and how best to use the information that you have been presented with.

This is the important part.

How do we use, and implement, our knowledge to create a better golf swing that will help us to score lower?

To begin with, I want to know that my students fully understand what we have covered in the lesson. Often, I'll ask a pupil, "Do you understand?" or "Does that make sense?" as my experience tells me that if a student is hearing but not truly understanding, they are far less likely to make the correct improvements.

I want to ensure they completely understand what I'm saying or asking them to do.

Sir Clive Woodward has a phrase, *"What, Why, and How."*

This is a great, simple way to check that someone has complete understanding.

This phrase could be used in so many aspects of learning and golf. For example, at the end of a lesson,

1. A student needs to have clarity on 'What' the subject of our lesson was
2. 'Why' were any changes important/relevant
3. 'How' to make any changes


To take a practical example, imagine we have been discussing statistics…

1. 'What' part of my game needs addressing?
2. 'Why' does this part need addressing?
3. 'How' will I work on it?


To help your understanding of learning – and to bridge the gap between the lesson, practice tee, and the golf course – I've asked Karl for his thoughts on this. Karl has had outstanding results in golf and he has a very practical approach towards learning and improving performance.

The first key question for me is, *how do we learn?*

The Oxford dictionary defines learning as: *Gain or acquire knowledge of or skill in (something) by study, experience, or being taught.*

Having read this book, you have been taught a technique and now have an in-depth knowledge that you can use.

Over the years, I've seen students respond very differently to the same information. This tells me that every student learns in their own unique way. As a coach, when I first meet a student, we need to decipher very quickly what's going to be the best way for that individual to learn. A coach must be able to adapt his style and methods of coaching and how to convey information, based on the individual in front of him. As a player, it's important to understand what type of person *you are* with regards to learning, to get the maximum improvement in the minimum amount of time. Having this understanding will help you during lessons but also when you're practicing alone.

*

**Karl.** The fundamental key to improvement is the age old wisdom 'know thyself' (Marcus Aurelius). Don't completely follow one specific person's way, hoping that what they do will automatically work for you. I don't think Aurelius was a golfer but his words are never more important or relevant.

We do not all learn the same way; we all process the world slightly differently and the key is to understand what works best for you. If you have responded well to video in the past then keep on using it; however, if you have used video and nothing has changed in your swing then more of the same is not going to change things. As another non-golfing genius, Einstein, put it, "The definition of insanity is to keep doing the same things over and over again expecting a different result."

A lot of interesting research has been done recently by Gabrielle Wulf into the concept of Internal and External focus of attention. If you are internal, you focus and have more awareness on your senses and the feelings of your body when you swing. You will be telling your body what to do by focusing your attention on a certain aspect of the motion.

If you are external, on the other hand, your attention is on the club, the grip, the shaft or indeed the outcome – the shot. According to Wulf's extensive work, she has revealed that many people would be far better suited to an EXTERNAL focus of attention, and I would suggest that all golfers at least have an appreciation of this.

In her experiments, when golfers focus externally they tend to learn better and more importantly are able to retain that learning under pressure. It may well be that an INTERNALLY orientated golfer could progress simply by switching the location of their focus. They could still try to achieve the same end goal (e.g. a better swing path through impact) but instead of focusing on a body part, they focus on what the club is doing. Again, all of this is about being your own detective and looking at the clues about how you, as a unique individual, learn best.

*

Typically, many golf instruction books have (in great detail) told a player how to move their body (internal) – often in very specific ways – but offered minimal detail about the golf club. It's why I have included and explained in such detail both SHOT and PRIMARY FACTORS (external).

For the more external learner, chapters 2 and 3 and the 'club' sections of chapter 4 will possibly have more of an impact on the way you practice. For a more internal person, the references of Hands and Arm, Lower body, and Upper body in chapter 4 will have more resonance.

I would now suggest you spend a little time experimenting to find your most effective form of learning: internal or external.

# Feel

On TV, in magazines, on the Internet, and in conversations about golf, I find the word 'feel' discussed so often. It sometimes appears as an almost magical or spiritual element within a golfer. It tends to get mentioned in two ways. Firstly, when a player is talking about a shot. For example, they may say, 'I lost my *feel* for the speed of the greens.'

The other is in a lesson, when they ask what a certain swing change or movement should *feel* like.

Our *feel* for the speed of the greens is completely individual and personal. It could be affected by what any player has been used to putting on recently, how well they are striking their putts, or even just the mood they are in.

In the second instance, a lesson, I wouldn't give an answer. I would get the student to rehearse the correct movement several times and ask them to register how it *feels*. That is then the correct feeling for them. How it *feels* to one player could be completely different to how it *feels* to me or another pupil. For example, we could be working with players A and B, on reference 5, and the correct thorax position. Player A may *feel* the correct position by the feel of their spine axis tilt. Player B may say they *feel* the correct position by the difference in the amount of rotation.

When you ask a player to describe the word, it's often very hard for them to accurately and easily do so. It appears to be a very personal and subjective thing. We seem to use it a lot in golfing language but do we really understand its meaning? Out of our five senses it's such an important one for practicing and playing golf and yet I find players often underrate it, and rely heavily on sight instead.

Sight and sound are factors when it comes to learning but shouldn't be over-relied on. Sight can be used to observe our swing, the strike, and ball flight. Sound is important for understanding the quality of the strike. It can also be a great help with putting. I often use it to get a player to wait to hear the ball hitting the bottom of the hole. Too often a player will just watch the ball, but following it with one's eyes straight after impact can sometimes cause technical issues with head and body movements. This, in turn, can have negative effects on the putting stroke.

*

**Karl**. We have five senses: seeing, hearing, smelling, tasting and touch. For the game of golf, our sense of touch, or feel, is perhaps the most vital. This is known as our kinaesthetic sense, our ability to feel what is happening to us in our current experience. If you suddenly focus your attention on the feeling of your feet on the floor as you read this book you are tuning into your kinaesthetic awareness.

There is a big difference between telling yourself to do something in a golf swing and actually feeling what is going on. Many golfers have their heads full of 'do's and don'ts' to the degree they don't feel what is ACTUALLY happening. If you can't feel what you are doing, it is tough to change in any way.

We often try to fix before we even feel. An example would be if I tried to put the club in a different position without first knowing where the club CURRENTLY is.

Many golfers would benefit by tuning their attention into what is going on NOW... before they try to change anything.

- Can you put your attention on the club head and keep it there all the way through the swing?

- Can you actually sense if the club is swinging out to the right of your target, or to the left?

Make some swings and hit some shots in what I call 'observer' mode. Simply observe what is happening before you try to change anything. As you tune into what is happening (as opposed to what you think *should* be happening) you will increase your sense of feel in the swing. When you can actually FEEL the club swinging left, you can then begin to work on feeling it move in a different direction.

A great drill to practice feel is the 'eyes closed' exercise. When we shut one of our senses down, we tend to heighten another. That is why feel can be increased when we close our eyes. A great drill on the greens is to aim to hit some long putts to the fringe of the green with your eyes closed. Stroke the putt and before you open your eyes call out "ON", "LONG", or "SHORT" to where you think the ball finished relative to the fringe.

*

One other way to gain a better feeling for where your swing currently is, is to combine one of your practice sessions with feedback using a TrackMan radar or 3D system. This will give you accurate and measurable information which can be allied with body and club feelings during your swing. When we don't have radar or 3D we can use a mirror effectively. Making correct, slow swings in front of a mirror – and consciously asking oneself what it feels like – is a great way to understand and improve.

# How much time do I need to put into my practice in order to get better?

There's been thought, and a lot of literature, suggesting that we need to spend huge amounts of time working on every specific area of our game if we want to get significantly better. But is it really a fact that we may need to spend hundreds or even thousands of hours practicing each area of our game in order to see significant improvement? Or can it be achieved in a far shorter time?

I believe (as I've said before) that the first thing we must do is target the correct area of our game for improvement (using our Statistics) then to have great knowledge about what we are going to try and do. This will speed up the learning and improvement process rapidly.

If I spend thousands of hours practicing with poor information, have an ineffective structure, or work in a manner not suitable for my own personality, it's certainly not going to be the best use of my time. If, however, I have good technical knowledge, the correct diagnoses and fixes, and an effective way to practice this information, surely I can make significant improvement in a relatively short period of time?

*

**Karl**. The 10,000 hour 'rule' [the idea that it takes 10,000 hours of deliberate practice to achieve expertise in a given area] is, for me, an overplayed concept that can actually be very detrimental. The idea that practice should be about 'time' CAN get in the way of progress. Just grinding out ball after ball often does nothing other than cement what is already there.

The absolute key to making progress is the quality of your ATTENTION.

Being aware and paying attention to what you are trying to do in your swing is far more important than the number of shots you hit.

Many people cannot keep their attentional focus for more than 30 minutes or so. So it would be my suggestion to work on different aspects of your game in 30 minute blocks of time. Work on your swing for 30 minutes then go to the putting green and work on another completely different skill, then spend some time in a bunker, etc. It is important that you change the LOCATION you are in, to keep your attention fresh. The walk from one location to another provides the brain with a break and you can then RESET your intention at the new location.

You will gain much more from this style of practice when compared to just beating golf balls on the range. The environment of the golf course is dynamic and ever-changing yet we tend to spend too much of our time hitting balls in the same environment in a very linear fashion. Always remember that golf is the ultimate RANDOM game and, as such, our practice time should reflect that. Give the brain the best possible chance to learn effectively for the TASK of getting a ball around a golf course.

Have you ever wondered why you stripe shot after shot on the range but then fall apart on the course? It's probably because you're practicing to be a good practiser and not preparing for a round of golf, says UCLA Professor Emeritus Richard Schmidt, a long-time authority in psychology and motor behaviour. Golfers should change tasks and goals with each swing, to create what is known as "random practice" he says. Most golfers train with "blocked practice" meaning they perform one skill over and over until they can do it without much thought.

"In blocked practice, because the task and goal are exactly the same on each attempt, the learner simply uses the solution generated on early trials in performing the next shot," explains Schmidt. "Hence, blocked practice eliminates the learner's need to 'solve' the problem on every trial and the need to practice the decision-making required during a typical round of golf."

After reviewing many studies on how we learn physical skills and writing the book *Motor Control and Learning - a Behavioral Emphasis*, Schmidt and research partner Timothy Lee concluded that random practice is much more effective for golfers because they have to "work the problem from scratch" every time they attempt a shot (just as they would on the course). Making the brain work harder to come up with a solution improves the retention of that skill.

In learning any motor pattern (full swings, chipping, pitching, etc.), the only time that blocked practice proves more effective is with rank beginners, Schmidt says. But once they learn the basics, random training is far more effective. Source: *Golf Digest*.

*

I would suggest trying the three stage way to practice a swing change below.

## 1. Block practice

As mentioned above, block practice is when you hit a number of balls, say 50, in the same way, from the same spot. With your full swing, I would suggest this type of practice is best done hitting into a net. For me the main benefit of block practice is to create new neural pathways, effectively helping you to change from one habit or movement to another. By hitting into a net, there is no emotional reaction or distraction from the ball flight. I know this may sound a little conflicting to earlier chapters in the book, however it's not. My point here is that, when on the course, the ball's flight is hugely important. However, when developing a new swing movement, not seeing flight can sometimes help. It can allow a player to focus solely on the internal/external feelings of this new movement and not get distracted with the resulting ball flight.

Remember, when we've identified an area of the swing that we want to change (based on our statistics and shot patterns) we need to learn how to perform the new swing movement. Having 100% of your focus on this new movement will help speed up the brain's ability to make it a subconscious pattern.

## 2. Serial practice

Serial practice is about short bursts of practice. You might, for example, aim at a specific target in reps of 10-20 balls, then change the task. This could involve changing from hitting 6 foot putts to 15 foot putts, hitting with a mid-iron to a driver, or a draw shot shape to a fade. This is almost like a halfway house between learning a movement and having an awareness of the outcome. For me it would be about building a bridge between learning the skill and being able to perform it.

## 3. Random practice

I often refer to this part as, target practice. Here I'm looking for a player to be 100% focused and aware of the shot's *outcome* (almost the complete opposite learning outcome to block practice). This part, to me, is the part of your practice that should mirror playing on the course as much as possible. You should use your routine and give the shot the same level of focus and emotion as if you were competing. There must be a specific target and intended outcome.

The other great part to this practice is that you can make it competitive, either against yourself or a friend. Having a competitive element can often be a great way to focus the mind and replicate playing in a tournament.

## Working on your swing changes on the practice ground

As a coach, I've often asked myself, "What's the most effective way for a player to practice a swing change they've acquired during a lesson on the practice ground?"

After all, you've analysed your game through statistics, ball flight, primary impact factors, and have the swing reference to improve. How should you take this knowledge and gain maximum improvement when by yourself?

*

**Karl**. If you are aiming to work on swing changes then one of the worst things you can do is go to the range, aim at a target, and swing at normal speed expecting the changes to take hold.

They won't.

Your brain will just return to the default of the old swing because the link with the target and your old action is wired into your brain. This is called Perception-Action coupling.

In effect, your perception of the target, and how to get a ball to that target, is linked – in your brain – to your existing action and the way you normally swing the club.

Here are two suggestions for working on swing changes in the early stages.

1. Eliminate/remove the target as it will only trigger your old swing.

2. Make the 'new' moves at slower speeds. Think of 'tai chi' and its graceful swirling movements. By working on your swing at much slower speeds, you give your brain the chance to re-calibrate and integrate the new move much better. The old adage of 'if you can't do it slowly then you certainly can't do it quickly' has never been truer than when you are working on your swing. Use video on the slower swings to see if you are actually doing what you THINK you are doing.

Once swing changes are established, it is essential that you test them during practice. Create game-like conditions of one shot, one club, to a unique target with scoring consequences. Make this part of your practice as close to the real game as possible.

*

Picking up on Karl's comments, above, on slow swings, I would recommend completing the swing at literally 20% of your normal club speed. Pay great attention to the exact references you make. Possibly check things in a mirror or use a video camera.

In turn, to cement the new, correct reference we are working on, pay attention to the specific thing you are practicing and then stop. Pause for a few seconds. In this time – if needed – look in a mirror and check that you are performing exactly what you want. This gives you a chance to really feel (either internally or externally) and understand the change.

Then, complete your swing and hit the ball.

After doing this for a while (20-30 balls) reduce the pause. Effectively what I'm looking for, here, is a process to check, reassure, and feel the correct position. As you build confidence, and the correct neural pathways, the pause can be reduced and this new movement and swing change becomes part of the sub-conscious movement to your natural swing speed.

# Separating playing and practicing

I remember one particular lesson I had early on in my coaching career very well. At the end of the lesson, I was certain the player understood exactly what, why, and how, I wanted them to practice. More importantly, using a range of clubs for the last 10 minutes of the lesson, the player was hitting ball after ball fantastically well. Neither of us could have been happier with how the lesson had gone. In fact, we were both rather excited as the player was about to go straight out and play in a medal competition.

At the end of the day, I bumped into my client and eagerly asked them how they'd done in the competition (expecting them to tell me they'd played great and scored amazingly). No! Disaster! My client played poorly and shot way over his handicap! How could this be? When I last saw him, after all, he'd hit every shot exactly as he'd intended.

*

**Karl**. It is important that, in practice, we aim to have a mechanism to practice exactly what we will find on the golf course. That means one shot from a unique place aiming at a target with a score involved. The switch needs to be from focusing on your mechanics to focusing on playing. This is where you incorporate the routine that you will use on the golf course.

If you don't practice in game-like conditions then you will keep going onto the golf course working on your swing. When you actually play, you then need to make a commitment to PLAY golf as opposed to just swinging the golf club. This involves an acceptance of less-than-perfect strikes with an ability to let go and move on from the outcome of any shot you have just played. The only place to get really good at this is *on the golf course*.

The problem with the range is that there is always another ball waiting for us to hit to make us feel good. The golf course doesn't offer that luxury. Many players need to take a long hard look at the amount of time they spend on the range as opposed to the golf course. On the range, you primarily learn how to swing… but it is on the golf course where you learn how to play the game.

*

This is a great observation from Karl. As mentioned before, we need to have time and various ways to practice our swing mechanics but we also need to practice – on the range – in the same way that we intend to play on the course.

It's important to have both of these practice sessions but keep them separate.

According to psychological research, there are four stages to learning a new skill. This theory of learning is a great way to understand why we need to practice and then play in certain ways. Unconscious competence is the ultimate place we are trying to get to – in order to perform at our best.

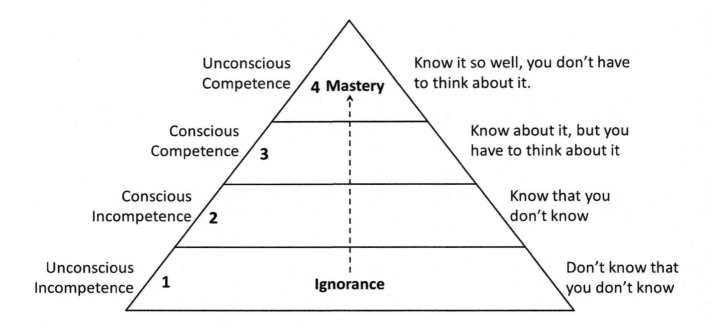

In golfing terms…

1.  Unconscious Incompetence – This is when a player is hitting balls with no plan or structure. There is unlikely to be a specific target or purpose to each shot. The execution level of the skill is also very low.

2.  Conscious Incompetence – The golfer has a specific plan and intentions for a practice session and each shot hit. The execution of skill has not quite reached a consistent and high level. It will take practice and repetition to move to the next stage.

3.  Conscious Competence – Repetition and practice behaviours then produce effective habits. The player's skill level rises as does confidence; they experience success and improvement.

4.  Unconscious Competence – This is where elite players live. They can perform a skill almost automatically. It involves natural automatic effort. A player will often be very external here. All of the learning and practice will have developed correct repeatable movements that produce the intended shots.

# Routines

When you watch golf on TV, or at a tournament, you might notice that all the top golfers have a pre-shot routine. Why? What does it do?

Over the years, I've noticed that professionals' routines are all slightly different and each has their own quirks or habits. The one thing that is the same, however, is that they are repeatable.

*

**Karl**. The real key to consistent golf lies not in your golf swing but in your pre- and post-shot routines. Unfortunately, most golfers are looking for consistency in the wrong place, the golf swing. You will never ever eliminate bad shots, your golf swing will always 'come and go' to a degree because of the human element.

However, we can become very consistent with both our pre- and post-shot routines and – perhaps surprisingly – the better we get at them, the more chance we give ourselves on the actual shot. The key to a good pre-shot routine is the ability to put your attention where you need it to be (i.e. on this shot, in this unique moment in time). We want to be in the 'here and now,' focused exclusively on the task of moving this ball to our target.

One of the most important things for the player to understand is how 'questions' focus your attention. If I asked you, now, 'What sounds do you hear?' – that question will focus your attention on the sounds around you. So if questions focus our attention then surely – as part of an efficient pre-shot routine – we need to ask GOOD QUESTIONS.

As simple as it may sound, just asking yourself 'What is the shot here?' on each and every shot, actually gets us to focus on this unique shot at this specific moment in time.

The question brings us into the 'here and now' and tends to drown out the other potential mental chatter. So make sure, as part of your pre-shot routine, that you ask good questions.

In terms of your post-shot routine, you need to be aware of your habitual reactions to shots. *Emotion* can be the golfer's arch-enemy to good golf.

- Do you get a little too jubilant with good shots and start making stupid decisions?

- Do bad shots affect you too much?


Just look back at some of your rounds and note your post-shot routine. Does it serve you well? If it doesn't, then aim to change it. This is a great opportunity for most golfers because you CAN have control over this part of your game if you CHOOSE to.

I see a routine being as personal as your fingerprints.

Let's focus on a pre-shot routine, in particular, here. For some it will last 5 seconds, for others 30 seconds. Some will be focused on external thoughts like taking a practice swing and feeling the desired strike on the turf, or trying to find a really specific target like a branch on a tree to focus on. Those who better utilise internal thoughts may try to control their breathing or have a swing feeling that they've been working on which gives them confidence for the shot. Yours needs to be right for you, whatever that may be.

I see the routine as a dress rehearsal for the actual shot. The routine is your chance to really dial in mentally to the shot and target before actually hitting the ball. Jason Day really looks like he's in the zone and absorbed by the target in his pre-shot routine.

I'd recommend a player having an imaginary line, say a few meters behind the ball. When stood behind the line, the player should be evaluating the lie of the ball, total yardage and carry yardage, wind strength and direction, elevations, ideal landing zone and possible hazards. This is the time and place to think about (and possibly discuss with a caddy, if you have one) the ideal shot and rehearse the swing you intend to use. This is the time to visualize the shot you are about to play and get a feeling for the swing. I wouldn't want a player to cross this line until they are 100% confident in what they are about to do.

Once you have crossed the line you are completely focused on the shot. Personally, I don't mind a player having a warmup swing or thought but it mustn't be a distraction, it must be target and shot focused!

## Focus during practice

It's so easy for a player to lose focus during a practice session. Sometimes it can seem like the harder you try and concentrate the less effective the session becomes. How can a player stay focused and get the maximum benefit from their practice time?

*

**Karl**. First of all, and reiterating what has been written earlier in the chapter, limit the amount of time you work on one particular aspect to your game! My own recommendation would be no more than 30 minutes on any element. So 30 minutes swing work and then, most importantly, change location. Walk to the putting green and do some work there.

One of the great problems with golf is that we play in an ever-changing fluid environment and then we tend to practice in a very fixed stable environment.

Also go with 'a plan'; what is it you are specifically going to do when you practice? So many golfers just go and hit balls thinking they are 'working hard'. Being able to work smart is a result of having a clear intention into what and how you are going to practice.

Play as many competitive games as possible when you practice. Even better, practice with a friend so you challenge each other (you are replicating the game because, in a tournament, there is always somebody there with you). The more you go to the range with a specific plan, the more you will be able to keep your focus and concentration. At the end of the session, you can walk away knowing you have done what you set out to do.

*

Karl's point about having a plan is crucial. If you don't have a plan, results from a practice session can become a lottery. By reading this book you should be able to form a clear plan; from Statistics to Shot to Primary factors to Swing references. Create a plan before the session and review it after the session. Writing it down, for me, is an essential part of the process. This way you can look back at your sessions, review how effective they were, and learn from them when planning your next session. Therefore the more detail you document... the better.

# Chapter 6
# Simple Secrets

## Using video correctly

A coach's ability to communicate with their students is critical to achieving success. The best coaches are able to communicate either verbally, visually, or kinaesthetically dependent on their students' most effective learning style. As a coach, it is vital that any message I attempt to convey is received and understood in the way that it is intended.

In my experience, the modern world of laptops, tablets, and mobile phones has hugely influenced the way we receive information and how learn from it; everything is very visual nowadays. More than ever, I see people watching and consuming content on their mobile devices. This is where video can be effective in capturing and reviewing a golf swing. Video is a powerful tool for conveying a message.

It can also be helpful in offering feedback when a player is practicing on their own. Through video, a player can reference relevant positions in their swing that they want to keep an eye on.

However, as we are all aware, pictures and video can be misleading. The two main reasons for this are the positioning of the camera and lens quality. When two cameras are positioned in two slightly different places, for the same shot, the results can look quite different. We may only be talking several inches of difference but these inches can change the look significantly. In turn, some camera lenses, especially wide angle ones, can create what is known as a 'fish eye' effect. This is where the video gains a very slight rounded, bowl effect, and such distortions can impact on what the player sees and interprets. This is why we would ideally have a 3D system as our referencing tool. However, I appreciate this often isn't possible, so video can be good as a general guide and to give feedback. You must be aware, however, that what you see on the screen will only be part of the story as it's only being shown in two dimensions.

My system when using video during a lesson is simple. I like to place the camera in three positions.

1. Face on
2. Down the line
3. Behind a player

From here I can see clearly all I need to. For each video position, I'd place the camera lens as follows:

1. Face on: Opposite and at the same height as the player's hands, parallel to the target line.
2. Down the line: position the camera directly in line with the player's hands looking towards the target.
3. Behind a player: have the camera centred upon the centre of the player's pelvis, parallel to the target line.

## Face on view

**(Left)** This view is good for looking at how the club, arms, and upper and lower body, are working together. The only lines I would draw on the screen, to help here, would be one down the centre of the head/face to highlight any lateral movements during the swing and one running up the outer side of the right leg to highlight any lateral leg/pelvis movement.

## Down the line view

**(Right)** This view, like face on, is good for looking at how all four areas (club, arms, upper and lower body) work together. This is the view where I draw the most lines. I'd put one running up the club shaft (this represents the plane board), top of the head, and back to the glutes, to indicate if there are any changes in posture during the swing. It is also worth adding one at the front of the head to highlight any sagittal movements.

### Rear view

**(Left)** This is a helpful position for watching the body without the arms being in front. The main areas to observe here would be the lower body and upper body. The lines I would draw on the screen to help here would be: across the top of the pelvis (to observe how this section moves during the swing), and on the outside of both legs to observe again how they move.

Referring back to my system when working one-on-one, I first review the ball flight then impact, both with a TrackMan radar. Then I look at technique, ideally with a 3D system and/or video. In doing so, I gather detailed and accurate evidence to support the plan for game improvement. Video comes at the end as it is best used for helping players to understand their movements and convey coaching messages (not just fault finding). It can also be used in a lesson to demonstrate the progress that a player has made.

## Optimizing your equipment

Depending on the club delivery data you produce at impact, a skilled equipment fitter can alter a few key things with your clubs to help you maximize your consistency and distance, and increase your accuracy. This will apply to both your irons and your woods.

The main areas they would examine would be launch angle, spin rate, ball speed, start direction, and centredness of strike. Each of these elements can be managed and improved by a skilled fitter. They will attempt to combine and manage all of these elements to produce an individual's ideal flight performance.

There isn't a set 'ideal' club that you can pull off the shelf; that's the reason club fitting is essential. You need to find yours. It is important to understand that when you change one thing, it can have an effect on another, and this is where the experience and skill of the fitter proves so valuable.

### Launch angle

Getting the ball to launch and spin correctly is the key to maximizing distance and accuracy. If the ball launches too high with the incorrect amount of spin (higher than optimal spin), it will lose forward momentum. Conversely, if it launches too low with the incorrect amount of spin for that launch (lower than optimal spin), it won't have the carry.

The main things that can be changed with your equipment to influence launch angle are loft, shaft type, and the centre of gravity within the head.

## Loft

Increasing or decreasing loft, by even just 1°, will have a direct influence on the launch angle of the ball when leaving the club face, and the spin of the ball. Both the launch angle and the amount of spin will increase if we increase the loft. The opposite would be true if we were to decrease the loft; both launch and spin will reduce.

## Shaft type

There are now a huge variety of shafts on the market for fitters to choose from. Regarding launch, the main specification to consider is the kick point. Shafts typically have a high, mid, or low kick point and it refers to where – along the shaft – it flexes. Generally speaking, a high kick point produces a lower flight, and a low kick point produces a higher trajectory.

## Centre of gravity (COG) within the head

Some modern drivers have the ability to move and adjust their weighting within the club head. Moving the weight around the head will change the centre of gravity. This will affect the launch angle and amount of spin the ball will have. Moving the COG between the front and back of the club head is what has the greatest effect on launch and spin. If we move weight forward and low, we can decrease the dynamic loft and the spin. Moving it back can increase both the dynamic loft and spin.

Manufacturers are pushing the boundaries of club head geometry to find the maximum amount of weight saving, in order to create more adjustability.

## Spin rate

Spin rate will affect the flight of the ball in terms of both distance and direction.

Excessive spin will cause the ball to climb too high and lose distance, and if the spin axis is tilted, excessive spin will cause the ball to veer off line. Managing the correct amount of spin is crucial. The main options a fitter would have to change ball spin would be: loft, shaft, how weight is distributed within the head, and ball choice (I'll discuss ball choice later in the chapter).

To reduce spin with the shaft, you may require a shaft that has a heavier weight or which has a stiffer tip. This isn't a guaranteed way to reduce spin but has the desired effect the majority of the time. As mentioned above, weight and the Centre of Gravity will also influence spin.

The ideal spin rate is partnered with the ideal launch angle of the ball and ball speed.

Often, on TV, you will hear a commentator refer to a shot that goes too far out of the rough as a 'flyer'. This happens when grass gets caught between the club face and the ball during the collision. This reduces the amount of friction between the face and ball, in turn reducing the amount of spin on the ball, and the ball therefore travels further than expected. Conversely, this is why a ball spins more from sand. The sand adds friction between face and ball, translating into greater spin.

## Ball speed

To maximise control with our irons, we want to achieve the correct balance between ball speed and spin.

For our driver, we want ball speed to be as high as possible to maximize distance. The main factors a fitter can change to help with this are: head type, correct COG positioning, and shaft.

Some heads are 'hotter' than others. The main reason for this is the Coefficient of Restitution (COR) which details energy transfer between the club and ball. Golf's governing bodies have now limited the COR to 0.830 which means that the maximum transfer of energy allowed from the club head to the ball is 83%. Generally speaking, all manufacturers are trying to get some of their products as near to this limit as possible using face thickness technology, different types of material, and even variable face thickness to increase ball speed from centre hits. Choosing a head that is close to the limit will help increase ball speed as more energy is put into the ball than with a club with a lower COR.

The Centre of Gravity position can be affected with clubs that have movable weight technology. A skilled fitter will be able to get these weights placed in the optimum position that will help maximize the transfer of energy.

Having the correct shaft for maximizing ball speed is crucial. Too heavy a shaft will not fully enable top swing speed. However, some players like the feel of a heavier shaft to enable them to be able to 'feel' the club during the swing. Also having the correct flex is a factor. If it is too stiff, the shaft will not 'whip' through, with accelerated head speed, which will lead to a lower ball speed. With a shaft that is too stiff, you may notice you launch the ball too low and the 'feel' at impact is dull/dead.

Generally speaking, the lower your ball speed when it comes off the club face, the higher the launch angle and spin you will need to get your maximum distance.

## Start direction

Some of the latest drivers have a system on the neck that can be adjusted to change the lie, loft, and angle of the club face. Getting this set in the correct position will, not surprisingly, help start the ball in the desired direction.

If the face is set to open at impact, the ball will start to the right; if it is set to closed at impact, the ball will start left. Earlier in the chapter, I wrote about movable weight technology and how moving this forward or back can have an effect. Additionally some clubs enable you to have more weight towards the toe or heel; this helps correct the spin axis so that a player who hooks or slices hits 'less' of that shape.

With an iron, it is generally accepted that a lie angle that is too flat will cause the ball to start to the right (when too upright, it will go left). The correct measurement here is the 'dynamic' lie angle. This is the measurement taken at impact not at address.

## Spin loft

I am sure you have noticed how your longer clubs (i.e. woods, 3 or 4 irons) curve more than your PW or 9 iron. To explain the reason for this, the first thing to examine is spin loft.

Spin loft is measured at the point of impact and is the difference between the angle of attack and the club's dynamic loft.

$$\text{Spin loft} = \text{Dynamic loft} - \text{Angle of Attack}$$
(assuming the face and club path are pointing at the target)

As an example, if we are hitting an iron with a dynamic loft of 20°, an angle of attack of -5° gives a spin loft of 25° (20° - -5° = 25°).

Spin loft plays a big part in curvature. What you can see from the first picture, below, is that both with the driver (and the 7 iron) the face is 1° closed to path. However the ball is finishing 8 yards left with the driver compared to only 3 yards with a 7 iron. This is because the 7 iron is producing a spin loft of 30° compared to the driver's 10°.

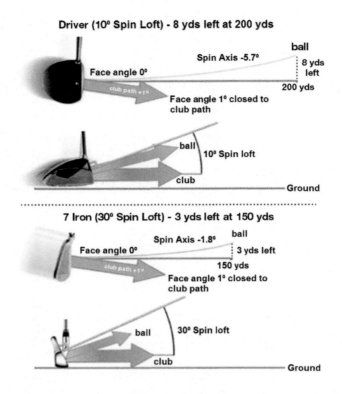

**Driver (10° Spin Loft) - 8 yds left at 200 yds**

Spin Axis -5.7°

Face angle 0°

ball

8 yds left

200 yds

club path +1°

Face angle 1° closed to club path

ball

10° Spin loft

club

Ground

**7 Iron (30° Spin Loft) - 3 yds left at 150 yds**

Spin Axis -1.8°

ball

Face angle 0°

3 yds left

150 yds

club path +1°

Face angle 1° closed to club path

ball

30° Spin loft

club

Ground

**Driver and 7 iron spin loft. Image courtesy of TrackMan.**

We can see on the next graph how keeping the face to path at a 1° difference affects the spin axis. You'll notice the line on the graph is not a straight line and that the lower the amount of spin loft, the greater the tilt of the spin axis and then the greater the distance the ball will finish from the intended target. Other factors that could affect this curvature include ball speed and spin rate.

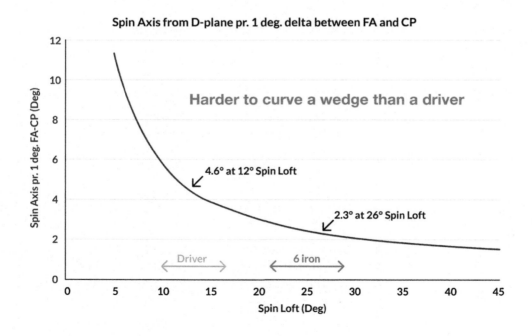

Spin Axis from D-plane pr. 1 deg. delta between FA and CP

Harder to curve a wedge than a driver

4.6° at 12° Spin Loft

2.3° at 26° Spin Loft

Driver

6 iron

Spin Loft (Deg)

Spin Axis pr. 1 deg. FA-CP (Deg)

**Why different clubs curve different amounts. Image courtesy of TrackMan.**

For the below we will assume you're a right-handed golfer with a mid-iron. For a left-handed golfer, the descriptions below will simply be the opposite way around. A (+) symbol, means to the right and a (-) symbol, means to the left of the target line.

## Hitting a straight shot

Hitting the conventional straight shot assumes a square face angle and club path towards the target and a centred strike from the middle of the club face.

As mentioned before, with a ball being hit off the turf, we ideally want to have a downward/negative angle of attack on the ball. This means I am making contact with the ball before the lowest point in the swing. You'll recall from chapter 3 (**See Left**) that making contact with the ball at this point in the swing would give me a club path that would be in-to-out (+).

Therefore, I would need to turn my (swing direction) left (out-to-in). This would need to be far enough left to get the club path back to neutral (0) and give the straight shot.

For hitting a driver with the ball on a tee peg, I would prefer a player to hit slightly up on the ball. Assuming a neutral swing direction, this would mean the club's path at point of contact will be slightly out-to-in (-). (**See Right**)

For a straight shot I would need to turn my swing direction slightly in-to-out, enough to get my club path back to 0 and hit the straight shot.

As an example of why I say there is more than one way to play this game, there are actually three ways to play a straight shot! The chart below clearly demonstrates how we can use what we learnt about gear effect in a positive way.

|  | Method 1 ("Classic") | Method 2 | Method 3 |
|---|---|---|---|
| Club path | 0 deg | Positive (inside-out) | Negative (outside-in) |
| Face Angle | 0 deg | Negative (closed) | Positive (open) |
| Impact Location | Center | Towards Heel | Towards Toe |
| Carry Distance | Longest | Shortest | Short |

Assumption: Right Handed Golfer

**Image courtesy of TrackMan.**

## *Playing the Straight, Fade and Draw shot*

**Straight shot - Standard "classic method"**
6 iron with a swing plane of 63°:

**Face angle** 0 Pointing straight at the target | **Club Path** 0 Pointing straight at the target | **Swing direction** -2.0 | **Attack angle** -4

NB: Your face angle is square to path.

**Fade shot "classic method"**
6 iron with a swing plane of 63°:

**Face angle** -2 Pointing left of the target | **Club Path** -4 Pointing left of the target | **Swing direction** -6.0 Left of the target | **Attack angle** -4

NB: Your face angle is 2 degrees open to path.

**Draw shot "classic method"**
6 iron with a swing plane of 63°:

**Face angle** +2 Pointing right of the target | **Club Path** +4 Pointing right of the target | **Swing direction** +2 Right of the target | **Attack angle** -4

NB: Your face angle is 2 degrees closed to path.

Method 1 is by far the preferred method for hitting a straight shot since this is the solution that will carry the furthest and is also independent of club and ball properties. For both methods 2 and 3, there are two things that the golfer needs to balance to create a straight shot. First, the club path and the face angle must be balanced to start the ball on the target line. Second, the ball must be hit on the toe or heel to compensate for the fade or draw that is created by the difference between club path and face angle. Our balancing act is dependent upon the club's properties, the friction between the club and ball, and the club loft. So, essentially, a lot of parameters need to be tuned precisely to offset one another.

## Wind

We all appreciate that playing into the wind (headwind) will affect the distance and flight of our shots. It's a complete misconception, however, that playing into the wind increases spin and playing downwind reduces spin. It's an incorrect belief held by many golfers.

The main point we should recognize when understanding the effects of wind surrounds air flow. Air flow is exactly as it reads, it's the flow of the air around a ball as it moves forward during its flight. The greater the air flow, measured in MPH, the greater the lift on the ball (which causes it to rise into the air) and drag (what causes it to slow down). When playing into wind we get an increase in air flow, hence the ball flies higher than normal and goes shorter. In turn, the ball will have a steeper land angle, so run less.

As an example, if we have a ball speed (speed of the ball measured just after impact) of 100mph and the wind we're hitting into is 25mph, then the air flow around the ball will be 125mph. When playing into the wind, greater spin would also be a bad thing, causing even more lift and drag. As a general rule of thumb the harder we hit a ball, the higher our spin rate, which is why it is better to take an extra club and swing easy when playing into wind. The effect of airflow will already reduce distance; adding spin by hitting the ball harder will only reduce it further.

When playing downwind, the opposite is true. If we had a ball speed of 100mph and a tail wind of 25mph, then we will have an air flow of 75mph. Less air flow means less lift and drag causing the ball to carry longer and fly lower. It would also have a lower land angle, meaning more run. Ideally we want to launch the ball higher in these conditions, as it would allow us to still have control of the amount of run by effectively increasing the land angle.

## Mud on a side of the ball

This has been debated for many years… how does mud influence a shot? The difficulty in predicting the outcome is based around *how much* mud is on the ball when the shot is played, as mud mainly affects two things: how the ball spins during flight due to mud covering the dimples, and the weight imbalance. If the amount of mud is significant, it will affect the centre of gravity of the ball. As a general rule, I would suggest that if there is a significant amount of mud on the right side of the ball, the ball will fly to the left (and vice versa).

## Tee height

Tee height will have two main influences: on your swing, and on the collision. As a standard, I would say around half the ball should be above the crown of your driver or fairway wood. With a rescue club or iron, the ball should be about ¼ inch off the ground.

Regarding swing, if you tee the ball lower you'll tend to encourage a swing that is more 'down' on the ball. As such, if you notice that you're a player who hits relatively steeply on the ball, you may prefer to tee the ball lower. Alternatively, if you're a player who hits a little more 'up' on the ball than standard, you may wish to tee it a little higher than standard.

Ensuring you have the correct tee height for your impact dynamics is crucial. You'll remember, in chapter 3, that we discussed vertical gear effect. Using what you learnt there, you can see the importance of making sure the tee height assists you in hitting the ball off the correct part of the club face. Generally speaking, with a wood off a tee, a golfer that hits too steeply on the ball will hit the ball off the top part of the club face, launching it high with less spin than the player who was to hit too much up on the ball; such a player would tend to strike the ball off the bottom of the face, launching the ball lower with more spin. Some golfers will, for various reasons, benefit from an impact either a fraction lower or higher on the face. Using all that you've learnt in this book, a little experimentation with tee heights will help you find the ideal tee height.

## Ball types

With so many types of ball on the market today, the choice for a player is huge. We have balls made up of two pieces through to five; some are higher spinning some are lower spinning; some are really hard, others softer. How do we know which one is best for us?

Again, the first point we need to understand is what our flight characteristics look like when we use a standard, premium ball. TrackMan radar would tell you this information. From here we can tailor the selection to your individual needs.

We'd start by looking at:

**Ball speed** - The speed of the ball just after impact. We want to maximize this for distance. Generally speaking, a player with a lower club speed will want a lower compression ball to maximize the compression/bounce effect from the face to maximize the ball speed possible.

**Launch angle** - The angle you launch the ball at. If you launch it too high you'll want a ball that has a slightly lower spin rate. Equally if you launch the ball too low, you may want a ball with a higher spin rate.

**Your spin rate** - The amount of spin your ball has just after impact. If you are someone whose impact characteristics create an excessively high or low amount of spin, you'll want a ball that has the opposite characteristics.

**Aero Dynamics** - The dimple pattern of a ball. The shape, formation and number of the dimples on a ball varies. The reason for dimples is to get the ball into the air; a ball with no dimples wouldn't get very airborne. Some designs promote a lower flight whilst others a higher flight. A general rule would be that the deeper the dimple, the lower the flight. This is due to the fact that the deeper the dimple, the greater the effect it has on the turbulence of the airflow around the ball. A reduction of airflow reduces the spin, causing a lower flight.

All of the above factors will influence your trajectory including height, curvature, and distance.

You should test flight characteristics using a driver, mid-iron, and a wedge. A ball will react differently with each of these clubs and you must ensure that you have the right ball for each of them. One ball may appear perfect for your driver but not for the wedges. You need to find the one that best fits across *all* clubs. Taking the time to ensure that you have the right ball will have an impact on your game and will contribute to that elusive reduction in your score.

Additionally, players often find a ball that they prefer the feel of on and around the greens. With this in mind, you should also test balls for chipping and on the putting green.

# Chapter 7
# Fixing Your Game

I remember hearing Jim Hardy at a seminar once describe how fixing your golf swing is a little bit like fixing a broken car.

You might have a car that for some reason just stops working. But, you don't want to change it for a brand new one; you just want to get it running again. It may be one tiny part of your car (like a battery or spark plug) that has stopped it from working. So, you take it to a qualified mechanic who runs the appropriate diagnostics to identify where the issue lies and then fixes the problem.

How does this translate to your golf? Well in golfing terms, someone may have been playing for 10 years, had very few lessons, and always played around their 12 handicap. Then, for some unknown reason, they've developed a destructive slice and they now can't score below 95. This person doesn't have the time, desire, nor sees the need, to change their complete swing but simply wants to get back to playing to their 12 handicap like they were a few months ago. By following the system of stats, shot, and primary factors detailed in this book, they can identify the swing issue with the help of the references listed, and find the specific fix to get their game back on the road.

As mentioned at the start of this book, *the best way to improve is to get a lesson off a reputable coach; their experience allows them to assess your game and offer practical ways to improve. However, the more understanding and knowledge a golfer has about his or her technique, strengths, and weaknesses, the more able the golfer is to help themselves.*

You must remember the purpose of this book, it's not to offer a 'one size fits all' swing manual. It's to help you fix your golf game, to help you play better golf. I don't believe any instructional golf book offers the one-and-only magical secret that can fix every golfer's game. Simply because there are over 60 million people playing the game, and every one of them will have their own technique. Therefore, there can't be a magical fix for all; it's not possible. What there is, though, is the science that underpins golf. This tells us how a ball flies and what we can do to control its flight. It is not the golf swing that dictates where the ball goes, it's the golf club. The golf swing is the vehicle to control the club. I'm not undermining how important the swing is, but we shouldn't get obsessed with how the swing 'looks'. Its purpose is to enable a golfer to deliver the club to the ball in the desired way, utilizing best practices of body function.

You need to be able to correctly identify your faults. As I've mentioned before, my ideal process is to gather accurate information using TrackMan radar data, 3D swing analysis, impact spray and video. All of these combine to offer accurate, factual evidence for identifying faults. Now I appreciate most golfers won't always have access to all of these systems, especially if you're practicing on your own. What you do have now, though, is the knowledge of what creates the ball's flight; this knowledge is the real golden nugget. This knowledge will point you in the right direction to fix your game.

Let's take a minute to recap how to use this book.

The very first thing I would like you to have done, before you go to the range, is to collect some stats on your game. These stats will point you to the area of your game that needs attention, and the fault to be looking for.

I will make some assumptions. Firstly, it's a long game issue. Secondly, that most people won't have a radar or 3D system. Most, however, will have a mobile phone with a video camera to film their swing as described in chapter 6. And it is easy enough to purchase either the impact spray I mentioned or impact face tape to see the strike pattern.

The next step is hit some shots and use the knowledge you now have on specific shot shapes to make a detailed observation of your exact, consistent, typical ball flight. You have your target line and you need to understand how the ball is flying relative to this. The questions to ask yourself are: What was the strike of the ball like? Where is the ball starting its flight? What direction is the ball spinning? What is the height of the ball? From this you can identify the exact ball flight from chapter 2.

Using the knowledge you have acquired for what creates ball flight, the primary factors will help you to look within your swing to see where problems lie. You should first identify where the ball was struck on the club face. This will then confirm any gear effect influences that could be a factor. From here, you can diagnose and understand the face and path relationship. You want to know, is it the face or path that's at fault. Remember, the face is mainly responsible for where the ball will start, the path will influence the spin axis. So, if the strike is centred and the ball starts left or right it, is the face pointing there at impact. If the ball is then spinning left or right, the club path will have been either left or right of the face.

Once you've identified the destructive issue, and why it's happening, you can now be confident of where to look within your swing to fix the problem to your golf game.

# Fixes

As we start to address some example problems in a golfer's game, let us take a moment to visit a hypothetical scenario and offer the best way to use this book.

## Stats

You've collected about 15 rounds of detailed data from your rounds and the stats have shown that the most destructive part of your game is that you're missing your tee shots 80% of the time to the right (and, on average, you're losing two balls per round because of this). This isn't acceptable if you want to achieve your scoring goals; you need to rectify this.

## Shot

You have gone to the driving range and hit a basket of balls with your driver. Upon closer examination, you have correctly identified that your shot to the right is a SLICE. The ball is starting close to your target line but finishing to the right of the target line.

## Primary factors

You have used foot spray on your driver's club face and understand that you are generally hitting the ball from the centre of the face. You now have the knowledge that the club's path is out-to-in (swinging left of the target at impact) but the face is generally square (looking at the target at impact).

You now fully understand that the face is pointing so far right of the path direction that it is causing the ball to fly in this way: a slice.

## Correctional process

Having re-read the swing preferences chapter, filmed your golf swing from the relevant angles mentioned in chapter 6, and with your knowledge of the primary factors, you have identified that the ball has been positioned too far to the left in your stance.

A knock on effect, at reference 1, from this ball position sees your thorax pointing to the left of the target and your thorax side bend being tilted to the left. Additionally, both of your hands are turned a little too far over to the left, in a weak position.

Coupling all of these things together, it is clear that reference 1 positioning was causing you to swing the club on a more vertical backswing plane (compared to what is ideal) rather than a plane that moved around your body.

This, in turn, led to your thorax side bend at references 5 and 6 tilting towards the target. As you unwound your lower and upper body around this thorax position, your hands, arms and club get pulled from outside the target line, across the ball to the inside.

Due to the fact that we are all built, think, and react differently, it's impossible to say if you set up with X fault, or have Y mistake in your backswing, you will then do Z (for certain) in your downswing. Golfers generally are very reactive with their swing, based on what they see the ball doing. This very rarely means they will find and fix the first point of failure during their swing. Most likely they will have a fault at either reference 1, or very early in the backswing, but leave it until late on in the downswing to make a reactive correction.

Two very important points I must stress once again are:

1. You must remember to fix the first point of failure, almost certainly at reference 1. I'd recommend reading this part of chapter 4 several times. I believe that all golfers, barring a physical reason, should have the ability to set up correctly regardless of ability.

2. You are very likely to create a swing that is based around what you see the ball's flight consistently doing. As a general rule, 90% of the time I find and fix a fault at reference 1 first, before changing a swing fault. As I've said before, the face is the most influential factor in determining where the ball will fly and I believe this often determines the technique a player adopts to compensate for any face mistakes.

Rather than trying to cover every possible combination of mistakes a golfer can make and offer a fix (as you can imagine, there are gazillions), let's cover the eight most common and likely scenarios to your diagnosed mistakes.

1. Heel strike
2. Toe strike
3. Bottom strike
4. Top strike
5. Face angle open
6. Face angle closed
7. Club path out-to-in
8. Club path in-to-out

The first four points from this list of eight are strike patterns, and the first thing you should do when you get to the range is to measure the exact strike of the ball on the club face by using an impact spray. You can utilise the sprays used to treat athlete's foot, and can purchase them from most chemists. Simply spray a small amount across the face of the club. It will leave a very thin layer of powder that will clearly show where the ball made impact on the face post-impact.

# 1. Heel strike

**Athlete's foot spray can show where the club
face made contact with the ball.**

## *Fault Overview*

A heel strike is when the ball is struck close to the neck of the club head, and is typically caused from two swing types: either an excessive in-to-out path, or where the complete swing circle moves further away from the golfer, outside of the ball.

Generally, over the years, I have seen far more people hit from the heel because the club is swinging excessively from in-to-out.

As the club swings into the ball, it effectively comes from behind us into impact and then moves away from us post impact. It is this movement of the club head (moving *away* from our body through impact) that causes the heel contact.

The other, less common heel strike, is when the complete swing circle moves away from the golfer, outside of the ball. Imagine a giant hula hoop around our body that we swing the club around during the swing. For a centred strike on the club face, the bottom (the lowest point of the hula hoop) is directly in the centre of the ball at impact. In this less common case, the whole swing circle has moved outside the ball. Effectively the hula hoop may still be parallel to the target line but it has moved away from the golfer.

**The red pane illustrates a down swing circle
that has moved outside the ball.**

If you've identified your fault as the club path being too far from in-to-out, please observe the notes later in this chapter (point 8) that cover the in-to-out path in detail.

If you've identified your fault as being where the whole golf swing has moved outside the ball, the following drills will help.

## Fix 1 (for both faults)

The first thing I would recommend checking is that you have the ball positioned in the centre of the club face at reference 1, and that you have a good posture which allows you to stand the correct distance away from the ball. Mistakes to address here are: the ball being too close to the heel of the club, or standing too close to the ball. It is worth reading reference 1 in chapter 4 again here, to ensure you understand and have the correct posture.

## Fix 2

At each reference in the swing, I would check that you haven't allowed your balance to move towards your toes. This shifting forwards of bodyweight (towards the ball) can push the swing to the outside of the ball. You need to ensure that you maintain your balance at the front of your ankles during the backswing and downswing and into impact.

**A player's weight correctly placed at the front of the ankles.**

A good way to do this is to place a tee peg in the ground under the correct balance points for where each of your feet will be positioned. These pegs should be in the centre of the feet, under the fronts of the ankles. Push the tee pegs almost flush into the ground so you can just about feel them under each foot when you take your stance. From here, take some practice swings, keeping focused on your balance points, whilst making the correct turn in the backswing and downswing.

## Fix 3

Another great drill for ensuring the swing circle doesn't move too far away from you (thus causing a heel strike) is to place a tee peg in the ground with about ¼ of an inch gap between the tee and the ball (and the tee between the ball and golfer). Address the ball as normal. To start with, make ¾ swings with a 9 iron trying to hit the ball *and* the tee peg. You should start to hit the tee using the club's heel and the ball will then be hit from the centre of the club head. This drill ensures your swing arc remains consistent through impact and doesn't move outside the ball.

**Hitting the tee peg from the heel ensures a
centre strike with the ball.**

## Fix 4 (for both faults)

For both the in-to-out fault and the swing circle moving outside the ball, you want to ensure your hand and club path is correct during the swing. For an in-to-out heel strike, the path is going to be underneath the plane. Rehearsing without a ball, and using very slow swings on a plane board will create the correct feeling. At the start of the backswing (references 1-3) ensure all of the shaft stays on the board and that it returns in the same way onto the front of the board as it approaches the ball during the downswing and moves into impact.

For the rarer heel strike, where the whole swing circle has moved outside the ball, the upper arms will often become detached from the thorax during the downswing between references 6 and 8. Keep a focus on the feeling of how the upper arms and torso stay connected.

## 2. Toe strike

### *Fault Overview*

Generally, and most commonly, a toe strike sees the club get swung out-to-in through impact. Just like the heel strike, but the opposite way around, the club is moving away from the ball through impact but this time closer towards the golfer. Because the club is coming 'into the golfer' the only part of the club head that can effectively reach the ball is the toe.

The other way I would expect to see a toe strike (but again less common) would be if the complete golf swing were to move nearer to the golfer. It's the same hula hoop analogy as a heel strike but this time the hoop would move closer to you. Again, the swing circle can be parallel to the target line but just nearer to you.

**This time, the red pane demonstrates a swing circle
that has moved to the inside.**

If you've identified your fault for a toe strike as the club's path being too far from out-to-in, please observe the notes later in this chapter (point 7) that cover this specific path issue in detail.

## Fix 1 (for both faults)

Like with a heel strike, I would check two points at reference 1. Firstly, that you have the club in the centre of the ball and that you're not addressing the ball on the toe of the club. Secondly, that you have the correct posture and are standing the correct distance away from the ball.

## Fix 2

To ensure your swing arc hasn't moved too close to your body, and to give you the correct feeling of a centre strike, I would do a similar drill to the heel strike but this time, place a tee in the ground so you have about a ¼ of an inch gap between outside the ball and the tee peg. As before, start by addressing the ball in the centre of the club head. With a 9 iron, make ¾ swings hitting the ball and the tee peg. Effectively, you should start to hit the tee from the toe and then the ball from the centre. You are working to ensure the swing circle remains consistent and doesn't move inside the ball.

**Hitting a tee peg from the toe ensures a
centre strike with the ball.**

## Fix 3

The next point to check is that you are maintaining the swing radius in order to hit the middle of the club. Often, people recognise that a narrowing swing radius causes the ball to be hit off the bottom of the club face. It may, however, also cause you to hit the ball off the toe. The image below shows you how a swing that excessively narrows in the downswing would cause a toe strike.

**The red curve demonstrates an excessively narrow downswing radius.**

Effectively, as the swing radius narrows, the elbows both hinge, move into flexion and the hands and club head come nearer to the body. As this happens, the club head can't reach the ball and the strike is off the toe. Often I see a player lose width in the backswing. From here, if they don't add in any compensations, the lack of width will remain in the downswing and impact.

To help maintain the correct swing radius in the backswing and downswing, try making a slow-motion practice swing with just your right arm.

Take your usual, correct, reference 1 position. Take your left hand off the handle and place it behind your back. From here, make your swing holding the club in your right hand only. Naturally, when a golfer does this drill, in order to support the weight of the club with just their right arm, they make a wider swing. Start off by making slow swings without a ball, trying to brush a tee peg placed in the ground. Once you're comfortable brushing the tee, with the new feeling of width, take your hold with both hands and try hitting a ball to recreate this feeling.

## *Fix 4*

Like the heel strike, but this time at each reference in the swing, I would check that you haven't allowed your balance to move towards your heels through impact. You can use the same drill as described for the heel strike's Fix 2, and place a tee peg under each foot, ensuring that you maintain the balance at the front of your ankles. Typically, I would expect this balance fault to occur in the downswing.

# 3. Bottom of face strike

## *Fault Overview*

There are two ways a golfer typically strikes the ball off the bottom of the face.

The first, shown in red on the illustration below, and typically the most common error for a strike off the bottom of the club face, sees the golfer strike the ball too far on the upward side of the swing circle. In this instance, the low point of the swing circle is several inches before the ball, so by the time the club reaches the ball it has begun swinging upwards. The low point being too far to the right of the ball can be caused by a number of reasons but the likely ones are a golfer trying to get extra loft onto the club, or their swing radius has got narrow on the backswing and they are trying to get the width back into it in the downswing (and have added too much). Often a player will feel too much of their weight has stayed in the right shoe at reference 7 and into the follow through.

Another less common reason for this type of strike pattern, shown in green on the illustration, is the opposite to the first. This time, the club's low point is too far to the left of the ball. This means only the bottom of the club head strikes the ball as it swings down, making contact with the ground several inches in front, and to the left, of the ball. This time the player may find an excessive amount of weight has moved into the left foot at reference 7.

**A low point excessively before or after the ball
can cause a bottom-of-face strike.**

To identify clearly which bottom strike fault you have, hit some balls with a mid-iron off a tee peg pushed almost flush into the ground. After you've hit a shot from the bottom of the face you'll be able to clearly see if your scuff/divot is excessively before (or in front of) the ball or tee peg.

## Fix 1 (for both faults)

The first point to check is that you have the correct ball position I explained at reference 1. This will be relevant for both types of golfer mentioned here (the ones whose low point is too far behind the ball, and too far in front). It is possible for a golfer to have a low point either too far behind or too far in front of the ball regardless of where the ball is positioned in their stance. However, the majority of the time, if you're the golfer who is having their low point too far behind the ball, I would expect to find the ball placed too far forwards in your stance, nearer the left foot. The opposite would be applicable to the golfer who has the low point too far left of the ball; I would expect to see a ball position too far forward to the left in a stance for this type of strike pattern.

## Fix 1 - Low point behind ball

This first fix helps the golfer who has been increasing their swing radius on the downswing.

As I mentioned before, this will commonly be for two reasons: the player trying to add loft to their club, or they have a narrow swing radius on the backswing.

This fault has often, in the past, been referred to as 'casting' the club head. Effectively and subconsciously the golfer casts the club with their arms on the downswing, like the action you would use for casting a fishing rod. This casting action excessively widens the circumference of the swing radius. You can check to see if this is your fault by videoing your swing from face on. From here, it should be clear to see if this 'fishing-like' action is happening on the downswing.

**(Left: The red club on this image shows the casting movement that widens the swing radius.)**

If this is your problem, the first point to check would be the club's loft during the swing. Essentially, you may have instinctively noticed the ball flying too low and worked out that by casting the club you can add loft. However, in doing so, the club's low point is moved behind the ball. Checking to see why there may not be enough loft on the club would begin at reference 1. Ensure the club is correctly placed on the ground and that your hold of the club is neutral. Typically, the face may be closed, pointing left, or the hold is in a strong position with both hands placed too far to the right.

From here, check at each reference between 1 and 5 that the clubface is as described in chapter 4. If it is in a closed position, it will be looking more towards the ground between references 1 and 3 and then, at reference 5, it will appear to face more towards the sky.

Another point I would check is that the right arm and shoulder are functioning correctly between references 1 and 3. Often, if the right shoulder elevates, or the right elbow doesn't hinge correctly, a closed face is encouraged.

If your club face is correct, then check to make sure you're not narrowing the swing radius in the back swing. The common way for this to happen is poor arm function. Typically, the right upper arm will have kept too much contact with the rib cage. This means it is then very hard to maintain any structure in the left arm, meaning it will hinge and appear excessively bent.

A great drill to help keep the width is the 'right arm only' drill. This is a similar drill to the one suggested for the toe strike's fix 3. Start by taking your setup but hold your club in your right hand only. From here, swing the club back to reference 5. You may find that you can't make as long a swing as normal; that's fine and correct. When you reach this shorter reference 5, stop, then bring your left hand up to grip the club. Because of the need to support the weight of the club through to reference 5, you'll naturally keep the right arm in a wider circumference. When you bring the left hand up to join it, the swing radius will be wider. When you do this drill, ensure you keep the club swinging on the correct plane around the body. Sometimes people can lift the club on a more vertical plane.

## Fix 2

Having too much weight in the right foot at impact can cause the club's low point to be too far to the right of the ball. This means the club is moving upwards as it catches the top of the ball.

To fix this, start by checking you have your weight evenly distributed at address. I would then encourage practice swings in front of a mirror to feel the correct weight transfer during the backswing, downswing, and follow-through.

Without a club, take your address posture. With your arms crossed, hands on opposite shoulders, make some practice turns back and down from references 1 to 7. As you do these practice swings, ensure you feel the correct weight distribution, both in the backswing and into reference 7. As you feel your weight transfer correctly, make sure you are creating it with correct pelvis and thorax rotation, both in the backswing and downswing.

## Fix 3

Another simple drill is to take a standard size business card and lay it flat on the grass long ways, about 3 inches behind the ball. Practice hitting a 9 iron; in the downswing take care to swing over the top of the card, so as not to disturb it (making ball-then-turf contact). One point to check is that you don't move your thorax too far left at impact, in front of the ball, in order to achieve this. Remember the image from reference 7 for the line of tension. This is the correct way to have your body, club, and arms arranged at impact to get a ball-then-turf strike.

## Fix 4

One of the other main reasons for a bottom strike due to the low point being behind the ball, is because the club path has swung too far from in-to-out. When the swing direction goes too far this way, the club will once again have its low point too far to the right of the ball, therefore it will be travelling up as it reaches the ball. If this is your issue, pay attention when you read point 8 later on in this chapter.

## Fix 1 - Low point in front of the ball

Typically, in this case, the player has moved their weight too far to the left side at reference 7 (impact). I would usually see this with the thorax being out of place at reference 7, and the side bend tilting to the left. Looking at the video of your swing from face on, you'll likely see your sternum and head left, in front of the ball at reference 7.

First of all, check that you have the correct weight distribution between the feet at reference 1. Then ensure that the thorax and pelvis are positioned correctly at reference 1. Your pelvis should be in the centre of the stance with your thorax side bend being slightly away from the target (6° - 9°).

From here, stand in front of a mirror without a club, arms crossed, hands on shoulders; rehearse the correct pelvis pivot, and start by ensuring that you don't sway to the right on the backswing. When the pelvis sways to the right, the thorax often compensates by bending to the left, towards the target. From this position, if you were to simply un-wind, the club head will get swung from out-to-in with the low point excessively in front of the ball. Having checked the pelvis pivots correctly, ensure that your thorax turns around the correct axis, established at reference 1.

Whilst doing this drill, check between references 1 and 7 that weight is correctly moving between the left and right foot.

## *Fix 2*

With a swing that has the low point too far behind the ball, I wrote how it's possible that the club's path through impact was too far from in-to-out. The opposite would be true here, it's likely this fault is linked to a club path that is too far from out-to-in. If you have identified this as your issue, please read point 7 in this chapter about an out-to-in path carefully.

# 4. Top of face strike

## Fault Overview

This is where the ball gets struck off the top portion of the club face. An excessive version of this is often referred to as a 'skied' shot with a wood. The club is moving excessively vertically down as it strikes the ball towards the top-line or roof of the club head.

## Fix 1

If a top of face strike only happens when off the tee, then the first thing (and simplest) to check would be the tee height. Possibly it's positioned too high. As I've said many times in this book, there's no 'one size fits all' fix and this is relevant here. Because all golfers swing the club slightly differently, they will all deliver the club into the ball slightly differently. Because of this, there will need to be a slight variation in tee height to suit an individual. With a driver, I recommend about ½ of the ball above the top of the club head at reference 1. For an iron, the tee should be almost flush into the ground, only about ¼ inch above the turf. If you found you're hitting too high on the club face (especially with a driver) you may want to check the tee height and lower it slightly.

## Fix 2

If it is not the tee height, then the main culprit is normally the narrowness of your swing radius. Imagine you are watching a golfer, facing them (e.g. they look up from their stance and look ahead straight at you). If you were to track their club head, you would notice – between references 6 and 8 – that rather than having a wide 'U' shape to the swing circle, it would appear more like a narrow 'V'.

**(Left: V (red) and U (green) shaped swing shapes.)**

A good way to stop this type of strike with a wood is to place a tee peg in the ground at the correct height for a driver; so about ½ of the ball would be showing above the club head. Place a second tee peg about 12 inches behind that tee peg and 1 inch nearer to you, this time with only ¾ inch of the tee above the ground level. Take your set up, then have some gentle practice swings, without hitting the ball, trying to brush the top of the second tee peg placed behind the one the ball would sit on in your downswing. Doing so will ensure you have a wider bottom to the swing circle and the club will make a more horizontal strike onto the ball rather than a vertical one. You should feel like you're now going to be sweeping the ball off of the tee peg. If you use a wooden tee, you can often tell if you're doing this correctly as you'll break fewer tees.

To help you understand and promote this 'U' shape, imagine trying to hit a nail directly into the back of the ball with your driver like the image below. Typically, with the V shape swing you would have been hitting the red nail into the ball. With a wider swing circle and a 'U' shaped swing through impact, the club will be hitting the green nail.

**'Nail' your driver correctly into the back of the ball.**

## Fix 3

For an iron shot, tee the ball up at the correct height. Place a second tee peg into the ground, about 4 inches behind the ball and ½ inch closer to your feet, and about ½ inch out of the ground. Practice making swings without hitting the ball, and try to brush this peg behind the ball on your downswing. Do it for 10 swings; create the feeling of a shallow, wider circle, and then hit balls off the grass as usual to recreate this feeling.

## Fix 4

Another very similar drill for irons is to place the ball on a very high tee peg, about 1 inch tall. Take a 7 iron and hit shots; focus on the feeling of sweeping the ball clean off the peg without breaking the peg. The key to this drill is to feel the sweeping action – a wide U shape at the bottom of your swing circle. If you get steep, you'll break the tee and be very aware of it (from the feeling of the strike of the ball, coming off the top part of the face). After about 10 balls doing this, remove the tee and hit the balls off the grass again; try to maintain the sweeping feeling.

The final four points from the list of 8 are club head patterns.

# 5. Face angle open

## *Fault Overview*

An open face angle is where, at reference 7, the club face is aiming to the right of the target line. Club face faults can often be traced back to the address position. It's crucial to remember how important the face angle at impact is, in determining the starting direction that the ball will fly. The face angle at reference 1 can also have an effect on how the player's swing then takes shape. It will potentially affect the shape of the golfer's swing by causing them to react to the direction the face is pointing, or by compensating for the flight that it is creating.

## *Fix 1*

To begin with, be very precise and consciously aware of how the club face is positioned at reference 1, before you take your hold. For example, if the club face is pointing to the right before you take your correct hold, chances are the face will return to the right at impact. In turn, ensure you have the correct lie angle of the club. If the club is sitting too much on its toe, then it will likely return to this position at impact causing the toe to dig into the ground. This momentarily slows the toe of the club whilst the heel keeps moving at its normal speed, thus opening the club face.

## *Fix 2*

Your correct hold of the club is crucial here. Now, it's not correct to say that if you have a 'weak' hold then you WILL have an open club face at impact. It's just probable and worth checking if this is your fault.

In such a situation, firstly check that your left-hand hold isn't too much in the palm with fewer than two knuckles showing. A correct hold will see your left thumb and forefinger at knuckle level. An extended left thumb below this knuckle can also indicate an incorrect placement of the handle across the left fingers and palm contributing to an open face. Check the 'V' of the left hand is pointing towards your right eye/ear.

Finally, with the left hand, ensure the pressure in the last three fingers isn't too tight.

Generally speaking, if the left hand is correct the right will most likely be correct.

I often find that an incorrect right hand is a reaction to a weak left hand. A weak right hand would see the handle positioned too far towards the finger tips. From here, the palm then sits too far on top of the handle. This can be identified by too many knuckles being visible when you look down at your hand at reference 1. In this case, it may be possible to see up to 3 or 4 knuckles and the 'V' on the right hand would be pointing further to the left, possibly at the left eye or shoulder.

The reason a neutral grip is important is that it replicates a similar 'natural' position that your hands will be in when you are stood up tall: arms relaxed and hanging down by your sides. If you look down at your hands when stood in this position, you'll notice your hands turn inwards slightly, showing about 2 to 3 knuckles on each hand. When you hold the club and swing at speed (into impact) your hands will want to return to this natural hanging position. If either of your hands stray too far from the preferred grip, the hand will attempt to get back to its 'natural' hanging position as you swing into impact. The shift between where you put them at address, and where they naturally go at impact, will either open or close the face.

## *Fix 3*

The key references with regards to an open face issue are:

Reference 3. Check that the face is close to parallel to the thorax. An open face would be more vertical.

Reference 4. An open face would be seen as the leading edge (or the bottom groove) of the club face, pointing left of the target line. Often, the left wrist can appear to have moved excessively into extension (i.e. 'cupped').

Reference 5. The face should be close to parallel to the left arm. An open face would point towards the ground, and the left wrist would appear to have excessively into extension ('cupped').

Reference 6. The face should be in a similar position to reference 4. If it's open, the leading edge will appear to be pointing left of the target line.

# 6. Face closed

## *Fault Overview*

Face closed is the opposite problem to face open; this time, the face is pointing left of the target at reference 7 (impact). As with an open face, a closed face at impact will determine the starting direction of the ball. A closed club face, just like with the open face at reference 1, can often lead to a player developing a certain swing shape at reference 1, or they may compensate for the flight that is created.

## *Fix 1*

Start at the address position, and ensure the club face is correctly aligned to the target before you take your hold. After checking alignment, ensure that the lie of the club is correct with the toe slightly off the ground. If the toe is excessively off the ground, it is likely to return to this position causing the heel to dig deeper into the ground. This would slow the heel down which would then cause the club face to close during impact.

## *Fix 2*

The next point to check at reference 1 would be the left hand. Typically, I would expect too many knuckles to be showing. Firstly, check the handle is correctly placed across the left fingers and palm and when the hand is closed you can't see more than 2 knuckles. It's also worth highlighting here that you need the grip pressure to be in the last three fingers. Typically, if the pressure isn't there, and it is between the forefinger and thumb, the face can rotate excessively through impact.

With your right hand, you need to make sure that the club's handle is not placed too far towards the palm of the hand. If it is, you won't be able to get the hand to sit correctly on top of the left thumb and you'll notice it sits more underneath the handle. Check that the handle is running across the fingers correctly so that when you close your right hand, it sits on top of the left thumb in the correct way.

Just like with the open face, ensure both 'V's are pointing in the correct direction.

## *Fix 3*

The key face references to check would be:

Reference 3. Check that the face is close to parallel to the thorax. A closed face sees the club face looking more towards the ground.

Reference 4. A closed face would be seen as the leading edge, pointing right of the target line. Commonly, the left wrist can appear to have moved excessively into flexion, often referred to as being 'bowed'.

Reference 5. The face should be close to parallel to the left arm. A closed face would be pointing towards the sky. The left wrist appears, once more, to have moved excessively into flexion.

Reference 6. The face should be in a similar position to reference 4. If it's closed, the leading edge will appear to be pointing right of the target line.

# 7. Path out-to-in

## Fault Overview

This is where the club path is swinging from outside the target line, across the ball, to inside the target line.

As I've mentioned before, I often find that a player will change their swing shape and club path based around the face angle at impact. In this case, if a player has been regularly hitting shots with a very open face, seeing the ball fly right, their instinct is often to swing, between reference 5 and 7, in the opposite direction (left) to try and correct this. Unfortunately, this makes things worse as the face angle isn't being fixed; the face angle direction and the club path's direction get further away from each other, causing an even greater curvature on the ball flight. With this fault, you may have also noticed that your attack angle has become a little steep and the low point – where the club strikes the ground – is a little too far in front and left of the ball; the divot may be deeper than it should, and the strike may be a little towards the toe of the club.

Essentially I see two different styles that can cause this.

There's set-up and swing shape A, where (between references 1 and 5) the pelvis will sway to the right, with the left hip dropping down, and the player's weight possibly moving to the outside of the right foot. To keep balanced, the thorax will bend towards the target rather than away from it. The player has a swing shape that is more of a tilt than a rotation. Because of this, the arms tend to lift and move on a more upright, vertical plane.

From here, because of the thorax and pelvis position, when the player unwinds from reference 5 into reference 7, the swing direction will likely be from out-to-in.

The other typical movement, swing shape B, is where a player's swing moves too far behind them in the backswing, between references 1 and 5. They tend to raise up out of their posture, lifting their left shoulder up. The swing shape looks more like a baseball swing, where the club is swung around the body ready to hit a ball at waist height. At reference 5, the thorax is more upright than at address, the shoulder plane is more horizontal than it should be, and the player's head has lifted and often moved a little to the right. The issue for the golfer is the ball isn't at waist height, it's on the ground! In an attempt to get the club to reach the bottom of the ball, the player throws the club excessively back out in front of them in the downswing. I would expect to see poor weight transfer in the downswing with the player leaving their weight on the right foot, using their right leg as their pivot.

## Swing A

### Fix 1

Looking at your posture position, these are the faults I would typically see and would advise checking.

The ball is likely to be positioned too far towards the left foot. This will then have the knock-on effect of misaligning the thorax. Having the ball positioned too far to the left in the stance will rotate the thorax left, opening it in relation to the target line, and the thorax side bend would likely be tilted to the left. You may notice this if your right shoulder is level with, or possibly higher than, the left. The head may also be leaning to the left and the eye line looking left.

I'd also recommended checking your foot alignment and pelvis position. Check that your lower body alignment isn't also to the left with your feet and pelvis. The pelvis may be tilted, so that the right hip is positioned higher than the left. Ensure your pelvis is in the centre of your stance, it's likely that you will have it more towards your right foot.

Due to your body being positioned in this way, it is likely that the upper right arm will be disconnected from the right side of the body. Check that you have the correct connection between your upper right arm and upper ribs. You may also notice that the right arm is extended. Viewed from down the line, you wouldn't be able to see (as preferred) the top of the left forearm above the right forearm.

Note: It is possible that your lower body is correct but the upper body may be as described.

## Fix 2

Once you are set up correctly in reference 1, we need to ensure you have the correct pivot. Having the correct pivot will then enable and encourage you to get your arms to swing correctly around your body, and on plane, for the back and downswing.

To get the correct pivot, I recommend standing in front of a mirror when rehearsing the correct movements.

Without a club, take your correct posture position for reference 1. Hold the top of each of your hips with your hands. Make a few practice backswing pivots and observe your pelvis movement in the mirror. Use your hands on your hips to feel the movement, and help ensure the pelvis rotates and doesn't sway. You'll also get a great sense of being able to keep both the left and right-hand side of the pelvis level. As you look in the mirror, check the right leg has maintained its position, the left leg hasn't collapsed, and the left side of the pelvis hasn't dropped down.

Once you're comfortable that the pelvis turn is correct, and you have a good feel for it, return to take your set up at reference 1; this time without a club, but with your left hand on your right shoulder and your right on the left shoulder. Pay extra attention and ensure that you have the correct thorax side bend to the right. From here, looking in the mirror, ensure (as you make a backswing pivot) that the thorax rotates around the side bend you set at address. Another good focus is to maintain the stability of your head. The slight tilt you should see at reference 1 should have been maintained as you rotate through to reference 5.

Once you're comfortable with isolating each of the movements above, try and rehearse them as one.

## Fix 3

With this fault, and as mentioned, you're likely to lift your arms too vertically on the backswing; from here, as you turn anti-clockwise with your body in the downswing, your arms and club come down from out-to-in. A common mistake I see, that can start this sequence, is the club face going back to reference 3 a little closed. This, in turn, makes it difficult to cock the wrist correctly. In an attempt to get the shaft moving upwards, a player will lift their arms instead.

Using the plane board here is a great way to get the club, hands, and arms to move away from the ball correctly.

**Use the plane board to check the correct face angle and create
the correct hand and club path.**

You're not going to hit a ball here, just make slow practice swings. Take the correct reference 1, and from here let the club head and shaft swing back, staying in contact with the board. As you do this, pay extra attention to the club face. As you can see, it is starting to rotate (middle picture). Ensure that the right elbow has begun to hinge correctly and the right shoulder is staying relaxed and has not elevated upwards. From here, continue to reference 3 (the right-hand picture). Check that the club face is only slightly downwards, close to being parallel to your thorax forward bend. An incorrect move will have seen the club face looking further down towards the ground and the right elbow won't have hinged correctly (causing the right shoulder to elevate).

From here, continue your pivot to the top of your backswing (reference 5). When at reference 5, you want to ensure that you have the left arm correctly placed, only slightly steeper than the shoulder plane. You can also check the position of the right arm, making sure it hasn't lost all of its connection to the upper body. Typically, the wrong move here sees the left arm far more vertical than the shoulder plane, and the right arm will have lost all of its connection to the ribs.

## Swing B

### Fix 1

The player may have a 'weak' grip that has caused the club face to be open during impact. Either or both of the 'V's formed by the hands are pointing a little too far to the left, possibly towards the left ear/eye.

At reference 1, I would typically expect a player to be more slumped over the ball in terms of posture, possibly with the chin tucked down towards the chest and a hunched thorax with weight through their heels. Accordingly, it's very hard to get the correct pivot in the backswing. Because of this, the player stands up so they can rotate the body.

You can use a mirror or video camera, as described in this book, to check both grip and posture.

I recommend that you re-read chapter 4, reference 1, which explains how to position both of your hands on the club correctly. Pay particular attention to handle placement across the hands and the direction the 'V's point on both hands. Also, re-read the section that explains how to arrange your lower and upper body correctly. Pay particular attention to the correct tilt from the hip joint and how the head is arranged. Whilst doing this, be aware of the need to have weight evenly distributed at the front of the ankles.

## Fix 2

It's very important to maintain your posture, most importantly the thorax forward bend as you rotate in the backswing, to fix this fault.

A simple practice drill here does away with a club and ball. Standing in your correct posture, with your glutes touching a wall behind you, cross your arms and hands onto the opposite shoulders. As you practice your backswing, ensure that your head and thorax don't move up and away from the (imaginary) ball whilst you keep your rear end against the wall. Effectively, this exercise will ensure you maintain your pelvis in the same place at the back of your feet whilst the forward bend in your thorax stays consistent. When you do this, focus on making the correct pivot whilst staying in your posture; be aware of how the level of your shoulders now feels at reference 5.

**A correctly maintained posture at reference 5.**

## Fix 3

In Fix 1, I mentioned the grip of either one or both hands. This allows the wrist to function correctly, as discussed in chapter 4, reference 2. In this case, if the wrists aren't able to function correctly because of the grip, I'd expect to see the forearms compensate and rotate excessively clockwise between references 1 and 3, causing the club head to be positioned too far below the ideal swing plane (too far behind the golfer).

Ensure you have the club placed correctly in your hands, then use the plane board.

Be very aware of keeping the club shaft and club head on the board as it moves back. As you do so, check the club face rotates open correctly, and the wrists have the correct function. This new wrist function may feel like there is a lot more movement than before, but this is okay, it's simply because there would have almost been none, before.

After the club head has reached reference 3, the arms will continue to swing around and up, and the wrist will continue to move. If you were to video your swing from down the line looking at reference 4, you would notice that if you were to continue the line of the shaft down towards the ground, it would point somewhere close to a place directly behind the ball.

**The shaft correctly on plane at reference 4.**

## Fix 4 - A and B swing

This drill can be used to get the feeling of the club swinging in the correct direction through impact, and can be used for both swing faults A and B.

To get the feeling of how the club head should correctly swing through impact and to stop this out-to-in movement of the club, practice hitting balls using two tee pegs like the picture below. You want to be able to hit the ball but avoid hitting the pegs. Place the outer tee peg about 1 inch outside the ball and about 4 inches back from the target. Place the second peg about 2 inches on the inside of the ball and about 4 inches towards the target. Start off making slow-motion swings with a 7 iron, only trying to hit the ball about 60% of your usual distance. Once you're confident you can do this (whilst missing the tee pegs) gradually increase the swing speed to your usual pace.

**Feel the club head moving in-to-out through impact.**

# 8. Path in-to-out

## Fault overview

Essentially, this is the complete opposite of the swing fault out-to-in. This time, the club head is swinging through impact from inside the target line to the outside of the target line.

If a player has been regularly hitting shots with a very closed face angle, seeing the ball fly to the left, their instinct maybe to swing (between references 5 and 7) in the opposite direction, right, to try and correct this shape of flight. As before, this would actually make things worse. By swinging the club head in this direction through impact, you may have noticed that your attack angle has become a little shallow and the low point has become a little too far behind the ball. The strike may also have come a little towards the heel of the club.

Like with the out-to-in path, I tend to see two types of golf swing develop for this fault.

The first, swing type A, is where the golfer has an upright golf swing on the backswing. Through playing and practicing, they have learnt that they can't successfully hit it from here so they try and flatten their swing plane on the downswing. Unfortunately, they overdo the correction and the club gets swung excessively from in-to-out.

The second type, swing type B, is where the swing shape has gone flat and rounded on the backswing. From here, a player maintains this swing shape and the club get swung in-to-out for one of two main reasons.

Firstly, because the golfer has, at some point, struggled to get the ball into the air; either consciously or sub-consciously they have tried to get the club to hit 'up' on the ball, effectively trying to scoop it into the air. This is a misunderstanding on their part as to how to correctly use the club to get the ball airborne.

The other reason sees a player slicing the ball (over years), so they've tried to set-up and swing from in-to-out in order to hit a draw. In this case, they've often had some lessons or read some instructional information but then taken the correction way too far.

For both types of faults, A and B, I'd recommend re-reading reference 1 before making any changes to your swing.

## Swing A

### Fix 1

The key areas to check at reference 1 start with the hold. Typically, I may expect to see the grip in too strong a position, where one or both the V's on each hand are too far around to the right, pointing towards the right shoulder. Because of this type of grip, the club will likely close through impact, starting the ball flight left. This then gives the player the instinct to swing from in-to-out to try and fix this directional issue.

I would then look at the posture. Typically, I would expect to see the spine in a hunched, rounded position. A major factor for the shallowing you have in your swing is a pelvic thrust in the downswing. We'll discuss this in more detail later as another fix. However, we want to find the first point of failure and a poor posture at address could lead to a player not pivoting correctly in the backswing, hence the lifting of the arms. From here they are also unable to pivot correctly on the downswing, making the thrust an easier option.

### Fix 2

Having checked against reference 1 in chapter 4, and fixed this section, the next area to focus on is the correct feeling for the arm and club plane on the backswing (reference 2 up to reference 5).

To do this I would repeat a drill I recommended in a previous fix: path out-to-in, Swing A, Fix 3 for club and arm path.

Using the plane board, I want you to do exactly the same as before. Having the correct feeling of how the club and arms swing on plane is crucial for you here. Not creating a swing that's too vertical will essentially take away the need to flatten the plane on the way down. Without this, the next Fix is far more instinctive.

## Fix 3

To stop the pelvis thrust that has caused the shallowing plane that then leads to the in-to-out path, we need to get the body to uncoil differently. Essentially, I want you to understand and feel the correct place that your lower and upper body should be at impact (reference 7).

Effectively, with a pelvic thrust, the pelvis is moving towards the ball. The brain's balance system kicks in and because the pelvis is taking our weight towards our toes, the thorax moves a little away and to the right of the ball. This then drops the club onto this in-to-out path. At impact, with this fault, you may notice on video that the body looks as though it is standing up and the weight has moved a little towards the toes. It's very unlikely you will be able to see, from down the line, any of the left-hand side of the body due to this lack of rotation.

Re-read reference 7 in chapter 4 to refresh your understanding of where the upper and lower body should be for this position. Begin by putting the ball on a small tee peg and take the correct reference 1. From here, without making a backswing, move your lower and upper body, and club, into the correct reference 7. You should now be in the ideal position for impact. Very slowly, swing your arms back about 2 feet on the correct path. At a very gentle pace, unwind in the correct sequence, clipping the ball away and swinging through again only about two or three feet. The key is to be able to feel where the lower and upper body should be as you *strike* the ball; focus especially on how the pelvis and thorax are rotating and not thrusting. Pay attention to the feeling of your glutes staying towards the backs of your heels, and your thorax covering the ball more.

## Fix 4

Another simple practice drill here, to give you the feeling of how you should maintain your posture though impact, is best performed without a club and ball. Stand with your rear against a wall in your correct posture. Cross your arms and have your hands touch your opposite shoulders. Practice making the correct pivot for the backswing and downswing. As you do this, pay particular attention as you correctly unwind your body into reference 7 that you keep your rear against the wall and that your head and thorax haven't raised up at all. Effectively, this exercise will ensure you maintain your pelvis in the same place over your feet whilst the forward bend in your thorax stays consistent through impact.

## Swing B

## Fix 1

I would suggest first checking your set-up; ensure reference 1 is correct.

For this type of fault, I would first check the ball position isn't too far back in the stance, closer to the right foot. Make sure that, for an iron, the ball is 4 inches inside the left heel and 1 inch for a wood. Effectively, a ball that is positioned too far back will close the thorax, aiming it to the right of the target.

The grip may be in a strong position where one or both 'V's are pointing too far to the right. This is another factor in closing the thorax to the target line.

From here, it's likely that you will have your pelvis positioned too far left in your stance. To compensate for this, the thorax is likely to be tilting too far to the right, away from the target. When videoed, from face on, you'll notice the right shoulder is excessively lower than the left shoulder.

When players have this excessive thorax side bend to the right, they may also notice that the left arm is disconnected from the upper body. Because of this, when viewed from down the line, you will see too much of the left arm on top of the right forearm. Check that you have the correct connection between both of your upper arms and upper ribs.

Stand in front of a mirror and check that the centre of the pelvis sits in the centre of the feet, weight distributed 50/50 between the left and right foot. The thorax will then have the slight side bend to the right I showed in reference 1, chapter 4.

You may notice that the head is also in a position where the eye line will be looking to the right of the target. With the head positioned in this way, it sub-consciously says to a player that's the line to swing the club on. The head should be seen from face on as a continuation of the thorax. The head should match the thorax side bend to the right but the eyes should still be parallel to the ball to target line.

All of these faults will be the start of a swing shape that gets too far around the player.

## Fix 2

In this fault and largely because of this set-up position, when a player makes their rotation in the backswing, they push their pelvis towards the target. As a compensation, the thorax moves further away from the target – excessively to the right. When a player maintains this pelvis-thorax relationship and unwinds anti-clockwise in the downswing, the arms, hands and club head are all beneath the correct plane.

What I'd like you to do here is to practice the correct pivot without a club, standing face on in front of a mirror. Similar to a previous drill, I want you to take your reference 1 position, arms crossed with your hands on their opposite shoulders. From here, watch yourself in front of the mirror making a pivot firstly to reference 5, then from reference 5 to 7.

Between reference 1 and 5, ensure that the pelvis rotates on the spot and the left hip doesn't move towards the target. The thorax will rotate but it won't increase its side bend away from the target. Refer back to the pictures in chapter 4 showing the correct pivot positions for each stage.

On the downswing, between references 5 and 7, again ensure the pelvis hasn't moved excessively towards the target and that the thorax hasn't fallen further way from the target. I'll often, in this instance, get a player to focus on keeping the pelvis and thorax more stacked on top of each other for both the backswing and downswing.

## Fix 3

The next part I'd get you to focus on is the way the club head, hands, and arms move away from the ball.

The best way I know of doing this is by using the plane board in the same way described for path out-to-in, Swing A, Fix 3. Doing this drill gets the club and arms to move away correctly. The only other part I'd like you to have an awareness of, is the amount and way the lower and upper body rotates clockwise between references 1 and 5. Typically, here, I see players over-rotate the lower and upper body, especially at the start of the swing. This over-rotation early on creates too much space for the arms and club to be swung into, and allows them to be moved behind the player early in the swing.

## Fix 4 - A and B swing

This drill is the opposite to Fix 4 for the out-to-in swing fault. Once again it can be used to get the feeling of the club swinging in the correct direction through impact and can be used regardless of whether you have swing fault A or B.

To get the feeling of how the club head should correctly swing through impact, and to stop this in-to-out movement of the club, practice hitting balls using two tee pegs like the picture below. You want to be able to hit the ball but avoid hitting the pegs. Place the outer peg about 1 inch outside the ball and about 4 inches in front of the ball towards the target. Place the second peg about 1½ inches on the inside of the ball and about 5 inches away from the target. Start off by making slow-motion swings with a 7 iron, only trying to hit the ball about 60% of your usual distance. Once you're confident you can do this (whilst missing the tee pegs), gradually increase the swing speed to your usual pace.

**Feel the club head moving out-to-in through impact.**

# Conclusion

If you want to fix your golf swing, you can now see how crucial it is to have a clear understanding of exactly what your ball flight is, and then what's happening at impact. This will then lead you to what you need to look for within your swing. It will direct you to find the origin of your problem within your technique. Identifying the first point of failure, is key.

Swing faults are all closely linked together and if you correctly find the first point of failure (highly likely to be at reference 1) this will have the correct and natural knock-on effect to fix other faults within the swing. That's not to say you only ever have to fix one thing in the swing. What I'm saying is this. Correctly identify and fix the origin of your mistakes; subsequent changes should all slot together simply. Understand and embrace the logical, clear path for making these changes.

Before you change anything in your technique, you must know it's going to have the desired outcome on your shots. That's why you must correctly identify the fault first, and that's the reason why I've structured the book in the order of Statistics, Shot, Primary Factors and Swing References. Too many people miss out some of these key stages, or focus on their swing first.

Now get out there, fix your faults, and shoot better golf!

# Other golf titles from Bennion Kearny

**Golf Tough: Practice, Prepare, Perform and Progress**
by Dan Abrahams

Golf Tough is an original and inspiring book– a golf psychology book that will transform your game.

Dan Abrahams is Lead Psychologist for England Golf, as well as a former touring professional golfer, and PGA coach. In Golf Tough, Dan offers you a powerful blueprint for improvement and a detailed plan for consistent high performance no matter what your standard of play. If you want to significantly lower your handicap, compete with greater consistency, win tournaments or reach the next level on the course, Dan's simple yet powerful philosophies, tools and techniques will help you break through your current barriers and reach your golfing goals.

Taking a unique viewpoint on performance and progression, you will learn from some of the top authorities in the game – the world's leading golf statistician, one of the premier coaches in Europe, a putting coach to the stars, and a former caddy who spends his days teaching players to plot their way around the course. This accumulated wisdom, combined with Dan's cutting edge approach in sport psychology – and with up-to-date scientific research, practical lessons, and eye opening anecdotes from golf and a variety of sports – makes Golf Tough the essential golfing read.

> Train your golf brain and your golf game to compete with confidence under pressure
> Learn about your two on-course controllers – self-talk and body-language – to play with certainty, focus, energy and intelligence
> Develop a golf game with a winning mental structure by creating world class pre-shot and post-shot routines
> Learn to plot your way around a golf course intelligently by understanding and grading risk
> Understand from golf psychology how the quirks of your brain hold you back, and learn tools to deal with distraction and a noisy inner voice

**A Round In My Mind: The Golfer and The Sport Psychologist on The Jubilee Course at St. Andrews** by Mark Wilson & Paul McCarthy

In this unique book on golf psychology and golf improvement, follow the fictional account of Chris Marriott, a 4-handicap golfer, as he plays a round of golf on the Jubilee Course at St Andrews – accompanied by a sport psychologist, James MacAndrew.

As each hole presents its challenges, Chris and James discuss their experiences of golf and Chris begins to understand what is holding him back from shooting lower scores and, equally importantly, better enjoying his golf!

Written by real-life sport psychologists Paul McCarthy and Mark Wilson, the book covers themes such as emotional control, decision-making, ego versus ability, removing self-imposed limitations, and controlling processes better. By the end of the book, readers will understand how to challenge and address the issues in their golf game that are hindering them.

A commitment to change for the better is a commitment that only you can make.

## Alison Nicholas: Walking Tall by Madeleine Winnett

Alison Nicholas, MBE, is one of Great Britain's most successful golfers. In a professional career spanning more than 20 years, she claimed 18 tournament wins including the British Open, topped the Ladies European Tour Order of Merit and, in 1997, won the most prestigious championship in golf – the US Open. Her aggregate ten-under-par total was, at the time, the lowest recorded in the history of the championship and led to her becoming The Sunday Times Sportswoman of the Year, and the LET Players' Player of the Year.

In turn, Alison is well known for her Solheim Cup exploits. She played in six, and captained the European team to a famous victory at Killeen Castle in 2011. Images of the team celebrating in front of the windswept castle have become iconic.

In this candid and entertaining book, Alison explores her years on both the LET and LPGA Tours, the ups and downs, her tournament records, her faith, and – of course – the Solheim Cup. Filled with anecdotes from the other side of the ropes, behind-the-scenes insights, and images from her private photo collection, the book charts the hard work, focus, attitude and good times that led to Alison Nicholas *Walking Tall*.

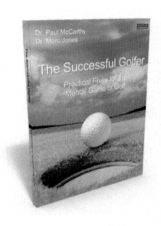

## The Successful Golfer: Practical Fixes for the Mental Game of Golf by Dr Paul McCarthy & Dr Marc Jones

You do not have to play many rounds of golf to understand how much of the game is played in the mind. Different courses, conditions, and shot requirements all present unique challenges that need focus and mental strength from the winning player. In turn, moving from the practice range onto the golf course can often magically produce drops in concentration, increased frustration, and unexpected self-doubt: drives go wayward, three foot putts get missed, and water features seem to become magnets.

The Successful Golfer is designed to help address 50 of the most common faults that players experience and which hold them back. These include: hitting the self-destruct button when winning, nervousness on the first tee, lost confidence, failing to practise as you play, losing focus off poor drives, and many more. Each fault is remedied with a clear practical fix. You will learn to develop effective practice plans, build a dependable pre-shot routine, cope with the pressures of competitive golf, and deal with distractions.

In the second part of the book, lessons from 30 fascinating research studies on golf are presented to help keep you ahead of the field. They include research on putting, practice, choking, and overthinking. In the third and final part of the book, clear instructions are provided on developing a number of highly effective techniques that can be used across a wide variety of situations. These include: pre-shot routines, breathing exercises, goal setting, and how best to practice.

*The Successful Golfer has now been adapted and reworked for short, sharp 20-minute golf lessons. There are six books in the series. Only on Kindle and iBooks*

Just some of what you will learn:
Learn to play consistently on the golf course and win when it matters most | Develop unshakeable confidence in all facets of your game | Build a consistent pre-shot routine to concentrate effectively and manage distractions | Boost your resilience and learn to cope with the demands of competitive golf | Uncover the golf psychology secrets of success from the world's best golfers.

Lightning Source UK Ltd.
Milton Keynes UK
UKOW07f1402210817
307671UK00004B/59/P

9 781910 515112